USS Philippine Sea

CV-47

Turner Publishing Company

Turner Publishing Company
412 Broadway • P.O. Box 3101
Paducah, Kentucky 42002-3101
(270) 443-0121

Turner Publishing Company Staff:
Editor: Bill Schiller
Designer: Heather Warren

Library of Congress Catalog
Card No. 00-101689
ISBN 978-1-63026-055-5

Copyright © 1999
Turner Publishing Company
All rights reserved

This book or any part thereof may not be reproduced without the written consent of Turner Publishing Company. This book was produced using available material. The publisher regrets it cannot assume liability for errors or omissions.

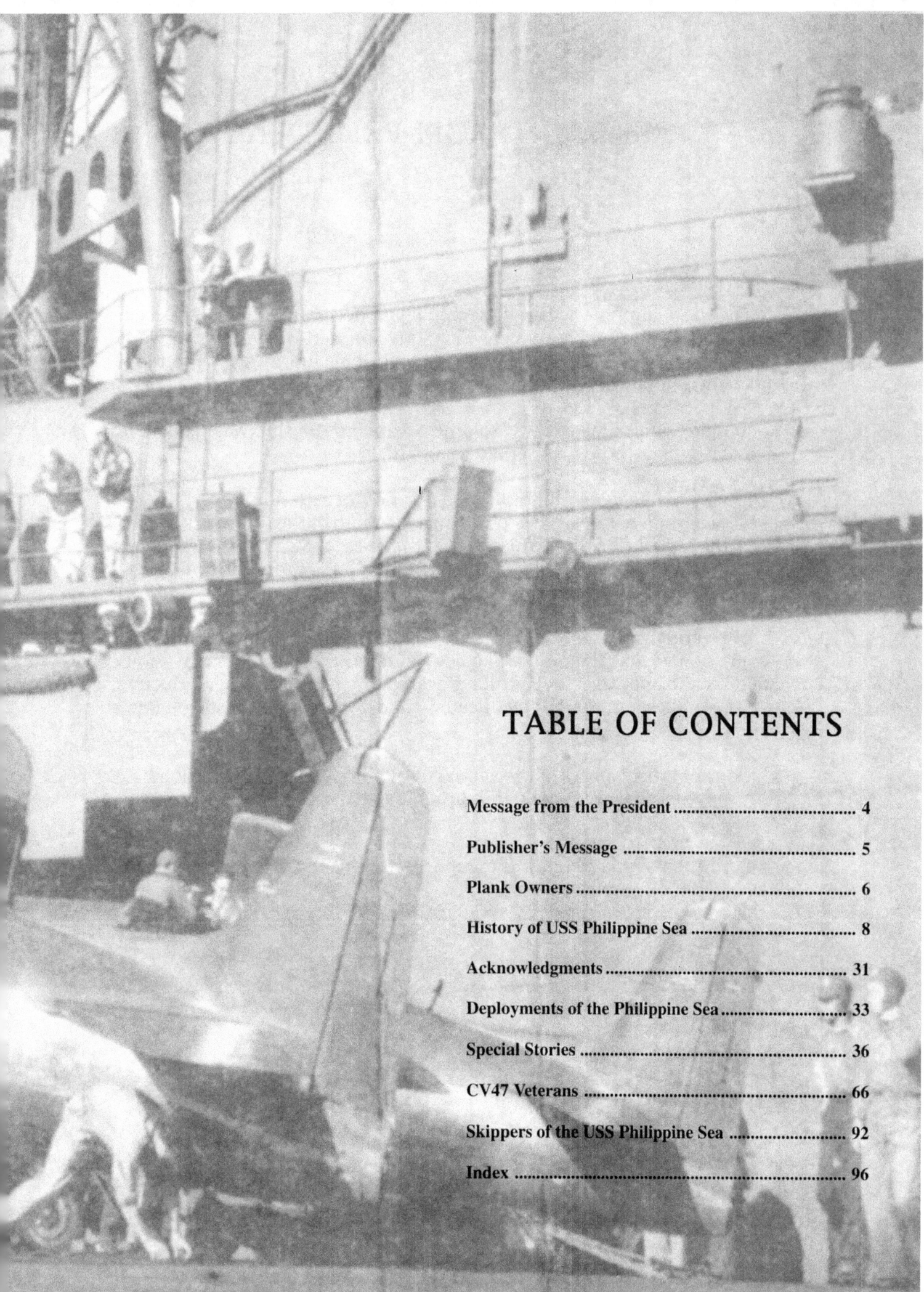

TABLE OF CONTENTS

Message from the President 4

Publisher's Message 5

Plank Owners 6

History of USS Philippine Sea 8

Acknowledgments 31

Deployments of the Philippine Sea 33

Special Stories 36

CV47 Veterans 66

Skippers of the USS Philippine Sea 92

Index 96

MESSAGE FROM PRESIDENT

The USS Philippine Sea as we served it was decommissioned on December 22, 1958 after twelve years of very active service. During this active 12 years, she logged an excess of 82,000 launches including 33, 575 catapult shots and a total of 82, 813 landings.

In March 1971 Phil Sea was sold for scrap and the ship was reduced to a "memory" for those who served on board.

The proud name of Philippine Sea was not forgotten however; in April 1987 the proud name was bestowed on a new ship of the line at it's launching - the Guided Missile Cruiser (CG-58). The CG-58 now caries on the proud tradition of the CV-47 - a different mission, a different concept but with the same sense of accomplishment.

The veterans of the CV-47 are scattered throughout this great country - some doing what they did when they entered the Naval Service - some have gone on to diverse "Fulfilling" careers. We have farmers, doctors, lawyers, policemen, firemen, educators, and congressmen just to name a few.

None of the members of the very active Philippine Sea Association have ever said that they were not damn proud to have served on so great a ship and so great a "team"

Both the Association and the Publisher thank those contributors who have made this publication possible.

Chuck Davis
CPO, USN (Ret)

PUBLISHER'S MESSAGE

The Battle of the Philippine Sea in June of 1944 has been regarded as one of the most dramatic and decisive of American victories during World War II. In a single afternoon, our forces succeeded in destroying over 400 enemy aircraft thus crushing Japan's hope of opposing our landings on Saipan. Navy Admiral Raymond Spruance reasoned that the victory not only provided us with the needed control of the eastern portion of the Philippine Sea, but ensured that our later landings on Guam and Tinian could go through without further Japanese naval opposition. As to the Battle of the Philippine Sea, Admiral Spruance would later reflect, "There was nothing else like it in the whole of World War II."

A little over a year later, the Navy commemorated the battle by commissioning what was one of the last of the Essex class carriers... a carrier whose crew stood as a living testamony to the strength and resolve of America's naval supremacy. Veterans of the USS Philippine Sea can take pride in the fact that their service and dedication was comprable to the grandness of their namesake. In preparing this history, the veteran sailers have echoed Admiral Spruance in their recollection of their years aboard ship... there was nothing else like it.

I am grateful to the many veterans who have contributed stories, photos and other material needed to make this book possible. Special recognition is reserved for Chuck Davis whose time, insight, and attention to detail proved critical in the ultimate completion of this book.

Dave Turner

Dave Turner
President

USS PHILIPPINE SEA PLANK OWNERS

The following list represents those who not only participated in the legendary battles of the Philippine Sea, but those who either helped put the USS Philippine Sea in commission or were attached to the Air Group at the time of commissioning.

R.C. Hill, AOM3
CHMACH G. Byland, M Div.
W.C. Decker, BM1
S. Rizzoto, ACMM
G.L. Williams, BM1
LTCDR E.B. Schiller
G.B. Williams, AETM1
A.A. Kropp, ARM1
R.R. Bermudez, Y1
Lt. R.E. Gallatin, VA10
R.N. Clarke, ACOM
C.N. Mayer, ACMM
A.C. Wilson, AMM1
C.C. Owens, AMMI1
LTJG C.H. Mundt
O.K. Birdsong, FC2
S.W. Gough, SSMB2
L. Miller, GM1
R.M. Evans, ABM3
LCDR Ace Johnson
LTJG L.A. Clarke
LT. J.E. Tefft, VF10A
G.N. Zivich, EM1
W.F. Uszenski, EM1
D.G. Clarke, AM1
J.H. Phillips, ACRM
LCDR J.S. Cooper, VA9A
LCDR J.N. Howell, Jr., VA10A
B.B. Hatcher, WT1
J.W. Jester, ACMM

USS PHILIPPINE SEA
HISTORY

THE FIGHTING *PHIL SEA*
AN OPERATIONAL HISTORY OF THE USS PHILIPPINE SEA 1946-71

by Robert J. Cressman as written in Fall 1988 Edition of Tailhook

19 June 1944 the Japanese Navy's Mobile Fleet made a desperate bid to interfere with the American landings on Saipan in the Marianas. U.S. naval forces, however, inflicted irreparable damage to the enemy in a battle that sounded the death knell of Japanese carrier air power. Paving the way for securing the Marianas, the Battle of the Philippine Sea, or the "Great Marianas Turkey Shoot," cost the Japanese three aircraft carriers, well over 300 planes and a proportionate number of trained pilots.

Two months later, 19 August 1944, the Bethlehem Steel Company shipyard at Quincy, Massachusetts, laid the keel for CV-47, the next-to-last Essex-class aircraft carrier. Originally CV-47 was to have been named USS *Wright*, in honor of Wilbur Wright, but the name was changed 13 February 1945 *to Philippine Sea*, commemorating the American naval victory.

While work on the ship proceeded, the war in Europe ended, and the Pacific war also came to a victorious conclusion. On 5 September

1945, three days after Japan signed the surrender accords in Tokyo Bay, *Philippine Sea* was launched. Mrs. Albert B. "Happy" Chandler, wife of the Governor of Kentucky, christened the new carrier.

RADM Morton L. Deyo, Commandant, First Naval District, turned CV-47 over to her first commanding officer, CAPT Delbert S. Cornwell, 11 May 1946 at the U.S. Naval Drydock, South Boston, Massachusetts, *and Philippine Sea* was placed in commission. Drydocked for two weeks, the carrier then fitted out at the Boston Naval Shipyard and sailed 13 June for NAS Quonset Point, Rhode Island. However, a shortage of men, a product of postwar demobilization, forced the ship to remain at Quonset Point in reduced operational status until that autumn. Underway 23 September, CV-47 conducted sea trials, returning the 27th to embark Carrier Air Group 20 and make final preparations for her shakedown.

Philippine Sea stood out of the waters off Quonset Point 30 September 1946 and commenced training en route to Norfolk, Virginia. On 1 October CDR Robert M. Milner, Commander, CVG-20, flying a Grumman F8F-1 Bearcat, made the first takeoff and landing on board the new carrier. Eight additional days of training followed, culminating at Norfolk. *Philippine Sea* departed for Cuban waters on the 12th where, from 15 October to 20 November, she conducted an abbreviated shakedown.

During this period CVG-20 conducted tactical exercises, one of which is recalled vividly by CDR Bob Buerger, USN (Ret), then a young pilot in VB-20.

The air group was making a coordinated attack on a towed spar about 500 yards astern of the ship. The basic plan was for the F8F-1s to come in low and fast to rake the target with machine guns and rockets to soften up the defense. The SB2C-5s followed immediately behind the last fighter, but from overhead in a steep dive, and dropped bombs. Finally the torpedo bombers came in low (and slow) to deliver the knockout punch.

I was the No. 2 dive bomber, so as a good follower I pulled into my dive on a two-second interval behind my leader. Unfortunately, he

Capt. D.S. Cornwell.

Mrs. Albert Chandler, wife of Albert "Happy" Chandler, Baseball's High Commissioner. Mrs. Chandler sponsor of the U.S.S. Philippine Sea when it was launched, was presented with the boatswain's pipe used in setting the first watch on the ship. Mrs. Chandler presented the Philippine Sea with baseball uniforms for the ship's team.

The Construction and Launch of the Philippine Sea

This photo was taken November 11, 1944 at Bethlehem Steel Company. It shows the beginning of a fighting ship. The port bow view looking aft records construction progress of CV-47 since keel laying 19 August. Originally named *USS Wright*, in honor of Wilbur Wright, the ship was renamed *Philippine Sea* on 13 February 1945. The name was picked as a tribute to the American naval victory over the Japanese Fleet of 19 June 1944.

Philippine Sea is launched 5 September 1945.

failed to see the last couple of fighters so we had a little melee at the pullout point. Luckily, the last fighter and I disagreed on our target lineup by several feet, but we were close enough to touch.

The vertical fin of the F8F went through the leading edge of my SB2C's left wing. Both of us could still fly, the fighter lost about the top one-third of its vertical fin/rudder assembly, but could maintain control down to about

90 kts, just a little above normal approach speed. The damage to my plane consisted of a jagged hole about 10 inches wide and a foot or so deep in the leading edge of my left wing.

I completed the pullout, and after regaining some composure, began to feel out the airplane. A squadron mate flew alongside to help look the situation over. My Helldiver flew reasonably well, except for some rather pronounced vibrations, until I slowed it down to simulate a landing approach. Below approximately 120 kts the airplane was literally uncontrollable with the left wing dropping despite all the aileron and rudder I could apply.

The decision was made that our damaged aircraft would be flown some 50 miles to Gitmo, to land on the runway rather than try a carrier landing. The fighter was able to land safely, but my adventure was not over!

Because of previous experiments with slow flight, I decided to not let my speed get below 125 kts. In touchdown at that speed, I landed a little further down the runway than I should have, but I certainly didn't want to take it around for another try! I tried to stop but couldn't use too much brakes for fear of nose over. Anyway, we were still rolling pretty good as the end of the runway approached, so I ground looped my poor old SB2C and it slid sideways off the end of the runway.

At this point there was no longer any control, and though the plane was moving slowly, it had enough momentum to straighten itself out before dropping off the 50-foot cliff at the field boundary.

There was no fire and the aircraft was reasonably intact, so my crewman and I were able to leave the aircraft unaided. Seatbelts and shoulder straps were snug, believe me!

In November *Philippine Sea* received orders to participate in Operation Highjump. Disembarking CVG-20 at Quonset before proceeding to Boston for repairs and alterations, the *Phil Sea* returned to Norfolk 29 December, where RADM Richard E. Byrd, USN (Ret), the technical advisor to Commander, Task Force 68, broke his flag 2 January 1947. Six Douglas R4D-5s with spare parts and skis, two Consolidated OY-1s, a Sikorsky HO3S-1, along with cargo and personnel, were loaded on board and the carrier stood out of Hampton Roads that same day, bound for the Antarctic.

Transiting the Panama Canal for the first time 8 January 1947 *Philippine Sea* cleared Balboa, CZ, the 10th and headed for a rendezvous with the rest of TF-68. Two days later she crossed the equator with entry into Neptune's domain accompanied by "elaborate" line-crossing festivities. On a more serious note 10 days later, the ship lost her HO3S-1 when its inexperienced pilot made an error in judgment on takeoff. Its crew abandoned the helicopter and was rescued within eight minutes.

After rendezvousing with the other ships

RADM Richard E. Byrd (left), Commander Operation High Jump, confers with Phil Sea's first CO, CAPT Delbert S. Cornwell, 8 Jan 1947 prior to JATO launching of R4D-5s off Antartica on the 29th.

One on deck, one coming in; note: blankets on wings to prevent icing.

of TF-68 on 24 January, the icebreaker, USCGC *Northwind* (WABG-282), was detached to Bay of Whales on the 28th to scout the pack ice and determine the "best suitable launching area" for *Phil Sea's* aircraft. She also took station on the track of the R4Ds to serve as a rescue vessel in case of a water landing short of "Little America."

Philippine Sea reached the approximate launch point and lay-to the 29th, awaiting favorable weather reports from Little America. It was decided to launch two ski-equipped R4Ds at the outset and hold the remainder until the first pair had landed and reported weather and field conditions. Word was received late in the day that the field was open for business and, some 660 miles from Little America, CV-47 worked up to 30 kts to get the required 41-kt wind over the deck, then launched two JATO-equipped R4D-5s. The first, piloted by CDR William M. Hawkes with RADM Byrd on board, was the first launch of an R4D from an aircraft carrier. Next day the carrier launched the other four R4Ds after learning of the safe arrival of the first pair. For the Douglas transports it was to be a one-way trip. After completing their mission of exploring and mapping vast uncharted areas of the Antarctic, they were abandoned on the ice.

When she received word that all planes had landed safely, CV-47 shaped a course back to Balboa. Transiting the isthmian waterway 22 February, *Phil Sea* got underway for Quonset Point, arriving 27 February. One month later the carrier embarked CVG-9 to resume her shakedown cruise. Underway for Guantanamo Bay the last day of March, the ship and air group operated together until returning to Quonset Point 5 May 1947.

In May and June the ship made two trips to Cuban waters conducting sea trials before arriving at Gravesend Bay, New Jersey, 1 July. Two days later she moored at Bayonne, New Jersey for preliminary work in connection with her upcoming overhaul. On 7 July CAPT George van Deurs relieved CAPT Cornwell as CO. On the 9th the carrier entered New York Naval Shipyard for repairs and alterations that lasted through the autumn of 1947. Underway 8 November she carried out post-repair trials and finished the overhaul at Naval Supply Depot, Bayonne, where she remained until 15 November. The rest of the year was spent in routine training out of Norfolk and Quonset Point.

As preparations to commence refresher training began, *Philippine Sea* again embarked CVG-9 on 3 January 1948. Sailing for "Gitmo" on the 5th, she spent most of the month in Cuban waters. After returning to Quonset Point she became the flagship for Carrier Division Four when RADM Ralph E. Jennings broke his flag 4 February 1948.

Following Second Task Fleet exercises the new carrier was ordered to the Mediterranean Sea 20 February for her first major deployment.

CVG-9 logged 8,534 flight hours during the tour, including 85 hours of night operations. Arriving at Quonset Point 26 June, *Phil Sea* disembarked ComCarDiv 4 and CVG-9. She proceeded to Boston Naval Shipyard for repairs to her catapult machinery where, on the 29th, CAPT John L. Pratt relieved CAPT van Deurs as CO. The ship remained in the yard until 21 July when she returned to Quonset Point.

Philippine Sea spent much of the summer and fall under the auspices of Commander, Operational Development Force, conducting experiments in carrier controlled approaches (CCA). This underway training involved both night and day operations for Attack Carrier

One R4D from the Phil Sea, flying only in Little America" vicinity did not use skies.

En route to Operation High Jump as they journeyed through the Panama Canal.

Philippine Sea is at anchor in Naples Harbor during Feb 1949 with VF-72 and -73 F8F-1 Bearcats visible on the bow. After getting a slow start following commissioning, CV-47 soon made up for lost time with an extended shakedown interrupted by Operation High Jump and two Med cruises between Oct 1946 and May 1949. She would deploy again one year later for the West Coast, and ultimately, Korea.

First R4D, piloted by CDR Wm. M. Hawkes, with RADM Byrd on board, launches from CV-47 660 miles off Little America IV (top) followed by aircraft number two with LTJGs Sylvester J. Linn and Wm. H. Martin and LT Geo H. Anderson as well as two NBC correspondents.

Shortly before taking off, Rear Admiral Richard E. Byrd tries on a rubberized cloth emergency suit in his plane. He took-off in the first plane to be launched.

Air Group Nine and a detachment from VCN-2. During the third quarter of the year, her pilots accumulated 750 hours and 670 CCAs, accomplishing 314 landings under simulated instrument conditions. Her experimental work completed, *Phil Sea* reported to ComNavAirLant 22 October. She then operated in the North Atlantic conducting cold weather operations, day and night maneuvers and battle problems, along the lower rim of the Arctic Circle, before returning to Quonset Point 23 November.

Soon thereafter the carrier began preparing for a Med deployment and embarked ComCarDiv 4, RADM Joseph J. "Jocko" Clark.

Philippine Sea, with Air Group Seven, sailed 4 January 1949 in company with *Midway* (CVB-41) and supporting ships, and reached Gibraltar the 13th. Reporting to Commander Sixth Task Fleet, CV-47 relieved *Franklin D. Roosevelt* (CVB-42) and began a series of exercises and port calls. Subsequent ops included exercises in waters off Libya, Greece, Cyprus and Italy. Steaming to Oran, Algeria, soon thereafter, the carrier pushed on for Gibraltar, where *Coral Sea* (CVB-43) relieved her on station 14 May.

During CV-47's second Med tour a joint operation was held with a British carrier, HMS *Triumph*. A mock strike was planned, with Royal Navy Fireflies and Seafires attacking *Phil Sea* and her escorts, while CVG-7 did the same to the Triumph force.

Not all U.S. pilots were required for the strike, and two found their way to Batt 11 aft of the bridge to observe the technique of their friendly enemies. The Seafires came in low very low and very fast. One CVG-7 pilot turned to the other with, "They aren't really low until they have to look up to see the fantail of a destroyer." Just then a Seafire, boring in and hidden from view of the carrier, rolled over the fantail of the destroyer on the port beam, completing the roll so close to the water that his prop sent up a rooster tail behind him. The two pilots just looked at each other.

Some of the British planes landed aboard *Phil Sea* at the same time some CVG-7 planes recovered on board *Triumph*. It was obvious to even a casual observer that, while the interval between the USN landings was considerably shorter than that of the British, the RN pilots were very much at home with their aircraft, both in the air and on the deck. The first aircraft to land aboard CV-47 was a Firefly piloted by LCDR Pridham-Whipple. It was stopped so quickly that its composite wooden propeller damaged one blade. When time came for the Brits to fly off, Pridham-Whipple called for his rigger, who sawed off the end of the damaged blade. He did the same to the other blades in the interest of balance. Pridham-Whipple then quickly took off and returned to *Triumph*, but not before the pilots and maintenance personnel of *Phil Sea* had exchanged some long looks.

After returning to Quonset Point the end of May, CV-47 proceeded immediately to the Boston Naval Shipyard, where she commenced overhaul that lasted through the summer. CAPT Raymond R. Waller relieved CAPT Pratt as CO 18 August 1949.

With Air Group One embarked, *Phil Sea* returned to the Caribbean that autumn for a post-overhaul shakedown. She spent the remainder of 1949 engaged in operational development projects with jet aircraft, CQs and task force exercises in the North Atlantic.

Winters at Quonset Point were often unpleasant; it was a long, cold walk from the air station's front gate to the carrier pier. But there were compensations, as the Quonset pier was relatively new and unobstructed. This arrangement allowed pleasant viewing of certain visitors.

Phil Sea was blessed with a damage control assistant very much on the ball. Even better, he was blessed with a wife who (according to one crewmember) "made today's Christie Brinkley look like an old crone." When the DCA was scheduled as command duty officer, Mrs. DCA frequently came aboard for dinner. As many of the duty section as could get away could be counted upon to be on deck for her arrival, her walk down that long pier and later departure.

By late December consideration was being given to having *Philippine Sea* deploy to the Pacific Fleet as soon as *Oriskany* (CV-34) was in service in the Atlantic. On 16 February 1950, however, the deployment date was moved up from the autumn to the spring.

During early 1950 the carrier participated in various exercises and conducted familiar-

Continuing her interrupted shakedown 27 March 1948, Phil Sea returned to Gitmo with CVAG-9. Photos below indicate variety of markings carried by her first air group during its three designations between 1946 and 1948. Below left: although flying F8F-1s, VF-20 used F6F-5Ps for their photo mission. Below right: The hottest thing in the fleet, the Bearcat could be hard to handle, as this VF-10A pilot learned. Center Left: VA-94 SB2C-5 (formerly VB-20/VA-9A) carries CVG-9'S "D" TAILCODE. Center right: VA-95 TBM-3E taxis forward after recovery. Bottom: CV-47 with CVG-7 embarked passes Gibralter 13 Jan 1949 on second Med cruise.

ENS Edw. D. Jackson Jr. is assisted from his VF-112 F9F-2 Panther cockpit by flight deck hands after his blind landing on CV-47, 17 September 1950. Jackson suffered severe facial lacerations when his plane flew through high tension lines in Korea. He was led back to the ship and "talked down" by his wingman ENS Dayl E. Crow.

ization cruises. Her frequent demonstrations of carrier operations for military and civilian visitors earned her the nickname *"The Showboat."* On 24 May she left Norfolk for the West Coast and transited the Panama Canal on the 31st, reaching San Diego 10 June.

Just 15 days later, 25 June 1950, North Korean soldiers smashed across the 38th Parallel into the Republic of Korea (ROK) and soon drove back Allied troops to a perimeter around the South Korean port city of Pusan. With the outbreak of fighting in the "Land of the Morning Calm," *Philippine Sea* received orders 5 July to sail for Hawaii and thence for Korea, with RADM Walter E Boone, ComCarDiv 5 embarked.

Before sailing, *Phil Sea* embarked Air Group 11: two F9F-2 squadrons (VF-111 and -112), two F4U-4B squadrons (VF-113 and -114), an AD-4 squadron (VA-115), plus detachments from VC-3, -11, -35 and -61. For plane guard and utility duties, the ship had on board one HO3S-1 from HU-1.

CVG-11 had not yet finished its training cycle, as VF-111 and -112 had just received jets. Arriving at Oahu 10 July the carrier conducted intensive CarQuals. On the 24th, RADM Boone hauled down his flag and CAPT Waller assumed additional duties as ComCarDiv 1 (Acting). That same day the ship sailed for Okinawa.

Anchoring at Buckner Bay 1 August, *Philippine Sea* conducted another change of command, as CAPT Waller was detached and CAPT Willard K. Goodney became skipper and acting ComCarDiv 1. On the 3rd, RADM Edward C. Ewen broke his flag as ComCarDiv 1, and on the following day, 4 August, *Phil Sea* joined *Valley Forge* (CV-45) and CVG-5 as a part of Task Force 77; destination - "somewhere off Korea."

Phil Sea girded herself for battle 5 August. In the wardroom RADM Ewen and CDR Raymond W. "Sully" Vogel Jr., CAG-11, addressed the pilots prior to launch. LCDR William T. Amen led VF-111's first launch, taking his men to sweep airfields at Mokpo, Kwangju and Kunsan. VF-112's Panthers, two divisions of four aircraft, likewise hit targets in the Mokpo-Kwangju area. VF-114's 12 F4U-4Bs knocked out a bridge, damaged two dams south of Iri and hit various targets of opportunity, such as warehouses, sampans and junks, on the way home.

Philippine Sea's pilots joined those from CVG-5 in flying combat operations against North Korean forces attempting to break through the Pusan perimeter. The carrier aviators conducted close air support (CAS) and interdiction of enemy supply lines as CV-47 operated off the south and eastern coasts of Korea. Tragedy struck VF-113 on the first day when, 15 miles south of Kunsan, two F4U-4Bs collided during a strafing run. ENS J.F. Kail crashed immediately, while ENS G.T. Farnworth nursed his crippled plane out over the sea, where he ditched to be picked up that afternoon. The next day, one VF-113 pilot pressed home his attack at such a low level that his Corsair took major damage from his own bomb blast but made it back to the ship and a safe landing.

On 9 August CDR Vogel flew with VF-114, leading a strike against the Riken Metal Company in Seoul; using 500-lb bombs and rockets, Vogel's flight hit the target "very effectively." Later that day, VF-114 and VA-115 teamed up to blast the marshaling yards and the Standard Oil Company warehouses at Seoul, leaving the latter burning, and knocked out several boxcars and a locomotive. That same day VF-113 Corsairs bombed, strafed and rocketed a factory at Inchon, setting it afire. CAG Vogel led another VF-114 strike 13 August, this time against targets near Pyongyang, the North Korean capital.

After replenishing at Sasebo 14-15 August, *Philippine Sea* returned to the east coast of Korea, commencing CAS for the hard-pressed United Nations forces and bombing key bridges near Seoul on the 16th. Next day VF-113 caught a 20-truck convoy with a cargo of artillery on the road south of Songjin and obliterated it.

At 1531 on 19 August, *Philippine Sea* launched eight F4U-4Bs from VF-114, led by Vogel, on a strike near Seoul. While the four-plane CAP element encountered no enemy aircraft, the four strike aircraft hit a bridge span with one 500-pounder on the first pass. Sully Vogel came around again for a second pass, but enemy antiaircraft fire hit his Corsair and set it afire. Vogel bailed out of the burning F4U-4B and pilots saw his 'chute stream, but it did not open and his body hurtled to the ground. Vogel was a little under a month shy of his 36th birthday; a veteran of aerial combat in the Pacific in World War II. He left a widow and five children. Although CVG-11 pilots destroyed the Han River bridge near Seoul that day, little solace lay in the feat. The next day ENS C.L. Smith of VF-112 died when his F9F-2, apparently hit by antiaircraft fire, crashed and burned near Sariwon.

Philippine Sea cleared Korean waters on the 20th and CDR Ralph Weymouth, skipper of VF-112, temporarily became CAG-11. The next day, as the ship lay anchored at Sasebo, a memorial service was held for CDR Vogel and ENS Smith.

CV-47 finished her replenishment at Sasebo 25 August and returned to the east coast of Korea. On the 27th, CVG-11 hit shipping in Wonsan Harbor, damaging what pilots claimed as a "destroyer escort" with rockets and cannon fire, and two "gunboats" by strafing. Between 26 August and 4 September, CVG-11 pilots claimed destruction of a "fleet-type minelayer" and four patrol craft at Wonsan. They conducted emergency CAS in defense of the Pusan perimeter, and destroyed key bridges along the North Korean lines of communication. *Philippine Sea's* aviators also discovered the enemy's major staging base at Kangge and photographed Inchon prior to the amphibious landing there.

Replenishing at Sasebo 5-11 September, CV-47 launched pre-invasion strikes in the Inchon-Seoul area 12-14 September and furnished air cover for the Inchon landings the 15th. In this bold thrust the First Marine Division took the enemy by surprise, captured the port of Inchon and, with the Army's 7th Infantry Division, captured Seoul and Kimpo airfield, severing communist supply routes to the south. Breaking the enemy stranglehold on Pusan, UN forces seized the initiative.

Between 16 September and 3 October *Philippine Sea's* aircraft furnished "deep support" of Allied forces and bombed supply routes and airfields from Seoul to Pyongyang, before retiring to Sasebo 4 October for a five-day respite. Early in this period, on 17 September, 25-year old ENS Edward D. Jackson Jr. of VF-112, while pressing a low-level strafing run south of Seoul, flew through high-tension cables strung across the Han River. His F9F-2 sustained extensive damage and he suffered painful facial lacerations and partial blindness. His wingman, ENS Dayl E. Crow, "talked" him to the ship and into the groove. The LSO took

VF-111 Skipper, LCDR W.T. Amen, became the first Naval Aviator to down a jet in aerial combat when he bagged a MiG-15 on 9 November 1950. In a usual practice of the era, Amen was flying a sister-Squadron VF-112 F9F-2.

it from there and brought him safely on board in a blind landing, as Jackson caught the number five wire.

An ominous portent of things to come occurred 30 September when VF-113 pilots sighted their first Russian-built MiG-15 jet fighter in the skies some 30 miles northwest of Seoul. *Phil Sea* resumed operations 10 October, providing air cover for the invasion of Wonsan, as well as bombing enemy supply centers and routes from Wonsan to Chongjin. Ship and air group returned to Sasebo 23 October, resting in Japan until November.

At that juncture, Chinese Communist "volunteers" swarmed south to aid the North Koreans. This massive intervention soon cut short *Philippine Sea's* stay in Yokosuka, and she sailed 6 November, rejoining TF-77 on the 9th. On that day her planes bombed bridges spanning the Yalu River and supply concentrations in Hungnam, Songjin and Chongjin. Over the next few weeks her planes, as well as those from *Leyte* (CV-32) and *Valley Forge*, pENS Edw. D. Jackson Jr. is assisted from his VF-112 F9F-2 Panther cockpit by flight deck hands after his blind landing on CV-47, 17 September 1950. Jackson suffered severe facial lacerations when his plane flew through high tension lines in Korea. He was led back to the ship and talked down" by his wingman ENS Dayl E. Crow. VF-111 Skipper, LCDR W.T. Amen, became the first Naval Aviator to down a jet in aerial combat when he bagged a MiG-15 on 9 November 1950. In a usual practice of the era, Amen was flying a sister-Squadron VF-112 F9F-2.ounded the enemy. On 17 November *Phil Sea* teamed with Leyte in dropping both bridges across the Yalu at Hyosanjin.

The Chinese Air Force introduced a new element to the war with MiG-15s. These enemy jets posed a serious threat to the prop-driven ADs and F4Us. On the same day that *Philippine Sea* rejoined TF-77, 9 November 1950, VF-111 encountered its first MiG and Skipper LCDR Amen (flying a VF-112 Panther), became the first Naval Aviator to shoot down a MiG-15. During November VF-112 encountered several MiGs, and the CO, LCDR John "L" Butts (who had succeeded Weymouth upon his permanent assignment as CAG-11) teamed with ENS R.E. Aslund in damaging one of the swept-wing bandits. Faulty guns, however (a common and vexing problem from the extremely low temperatures at altitude), robbed Butts and Aslund of a kill.

On 26 November, Chinese Communist forces smashed into the "greatly extended" UN forces in a surprise assault, driving a deep wedge between Eighth Army and Tenth Corps. The specter of isolation and annihilation loomed large as Allied troops pulled back before the enemy onslaught. Between 2 and 25 December *Philippine Sea's* planes conducted close air support in the Chosin Reservoir area, covering the successful extraction of friendly forces (most notably the First Marine Division) to Hungnam and evacuation. Completing these operations on Christmas Day, *Phil Sea* reached Sasebo on the 26th, remaining until 7 January 1951.

On 8 January *Philippine Sea* rejoined TF-77 and supported UN operations around the 38th Parallel, attacking enemy supply routes on the east coast of Korea until 1 February. Detached that day, the carrier reached Yokosuka the 3rd for a week's sojourn. Back at work 12 February the carrier again operated off Korea's east coast, providing interdiction and CAS until 13 March. During this period, on 25 February, RADM Ewen transferred his flag at sea to *Valley Forge*, and CAPT Ira E. Hobbs relieved CAPT Goodney as CV-47's CO.

Philippine Sea returned to Yokosuka 17 March and soon began an air group change. Between 26 March and 2 April the ship offloaded aircraft and disembarked men of CVG-11 and took aboard planes and personnel of Air Group Two from *Valley Forge*. Departing for Korea once more, *Phil Sea* had on board three F4U-4 squadrons (VF-24, -63 and -64) and an AD-2 unit (VA-65), as well as the usual composite squadron detachments.

Rejoining TF-77 on 4 April, *Philippine Sea,* with VADM Harold M. "Beauty" Martin, Com7thFlt embarked, resumed operations in the Sea of Japan until the 8th, when she and her screen sailed for Formosa to counter Red Chinese threats against the island. After a show of force off the Chinese coast and over the northern part of Formosa 11-13 April, CV-47 returned north giving support to UN ground forces between 16 April and 3 May. Detached from TF-77 on the latter date, she returned to

Yokosuka three days later where VADM Martin transferred his flag to New Jersey (BB-62). The North Korean spring offensive, however, soon pulled *Phil Sea* back to the line. During 17-30 May she furnished close air support for the continually hard-pressed UN forces.

She then detached from TF-77 on 30 May and departed for home 2 June. Crossing the 180th meridian on the fifth, the carrier passed beneath the Golden Gate Bridge 9 June, a 3,200-foot "homeward bound" pennant trailing in her wake. She had bettered *Boxer's* (CV-21) transpacific crossing mark by five-and-a-half hours, and moored at NAS Alameda to a tumultuous welcome. Following a quick trip to San Diego, she sailed for Hunter's Point Naval Shipyard at San Francisco, arriving 21 June, nearly one year after her hasty departure for the war zone.

Philippine Sea had amassed impressive statistics during her first Korean War deployment, a feat made more impressive because prior to entering combat flying, her air group was comparatively untrained and its two jet squadrons were breaking in new aircraft. During 11 months of operations CV-47 had conducted 7,627 offensive sorties, 2,660 defensive, and 1,856 "miscellaneous." She had expended 5,985 tons of bombs and rockets, 1,335 tons of napalm, and 2,747,000 rounds of machine gun or cannon ammunition. Her close air support had been delivered in areas ranging from a few miles in advance of the front lines to only a few hundred yards.

Upon completion of her overhaul at Hunter's Point, CV-47 conducted CarQuals in the San Diego area through the autumn and into the winter of 1951. Again, with CVG-11

Navy experiment involving blimp.

(minus VF-111) embarked, she sailed for the Far East 31 December.

Ship and air group conducted training en route, and spent 7-11 January 1952 with further training in the Hawaiian operating area. Exercising subsequently with Destroyer Division 92, her screen for the voyage, *Philippine Sea* reached Yokosuka 20 January then rejoined TF 77 on 3 February.

CV-47 welcomed a new skipper when CAPT Allen Smith Jr. relieved CAPT Hobbs 4 February. From 4-20 February *Philippine Sea* launched nearly continuous air strikes in an effort to impede North Korean railroad traffic. Other frequent targets for the nearly 450 tons of ordnance expended during this period included transportation, communications, industrial, and supply facilities. Only a task force replenishment or inclement weather kept aircraft idle and then only for short periods of time.

Phil Sea was in Yokosuka from 22 February to 17 March, where her officers and men enjoyed rest and recreation while the ship got a needed bit of upkeep. On 11 March RADM Apollo Soucek, ComCarDiv 3, and his staff came on board, making *Philippine Sea* a flagship once more. Rejoining TF-77 the 19th, she resumed her interdiction and close air support tasks the following day. During this period CVG-11 expended approximately 1,200 tons of bombs, rockets and machine gun ammunition.

Philippine Sea detached from TF-77 16 April and repaired to Yokosuka where she spent the next 27 days. Resuming operations 14 May, the carrier launched strikes the following day. Between mid-May and 4 June, CV-47 hurled 1,180 sorties against the enemy, in the perennial effort to interdict communist transportation and communications. She also hammered industrial and supply facilities, paying special attention to the North Korean railroad system. After a visit to Yokosuka, she conducted CarQuals on the 16th for McDonnell F2H-2P Banshees, which now equipped part of VC-61. Before the ship left Japanese waters, VADM Jocko Clark, Com7thFlt, embarked 20 June to observe operations. The following day *Phil Sea* sailed to rejoin TF-77 as Seventh Fleet flagship.

By that point, the Korean War had been dragging on for two years, and one year of truce talks at Panmunjom had accomplished nothing. Negotiating a cease fire with the communists did not appear likely, nor did the prospect of invading and subduing North Korea. The war appeared stalemated and the interdiction campaign against enemy supply traffic appeared to be something less than a success. Such efforts had mired into dull routine, day in and day out, described as "ceaseless and unspectacular" duty.

The most coveted targets, North Korean hydro-electric power plants along the Chinese border, lay untouched. The Joint Chiefs of Staff (JCS) had placed these Yalu River powerplants out of bounds in the war. Hoping to occupy North Korea and avoid needless destruction to be made good in reconstruction of the conquered enemy's homeland, the plants had not been bombed. After the daring landing at Inchon in September, the plants had been spared to deny the Chinese an excuse for intervening; after China did enter the war, the plants were not bombed so as not to "prejudice the course of the armistice negotiations."

By the time *Philippine Sea* was on her way back to TF-77, the Commander in Chief, Far East, GEN Mark Clark, had decided upon something that would "make the communists realize that we are still fighting." Since the powerplants along the Yalu provided electrical power to run the enemy's radar network and factories, Clark decided that those key hydroelectric works had to be put out of action. He informed the JCS of his intentions with a detailed plan of attack. Upon JCS approval of the mission, VADM Clark in Tokyo did not hesitate to venture his opinion that bombing the hydroelectric works at Suiho, a major source of power for Manchurian industry, was a "Navy job." He offered 36 Skyraiders, each armed with a 5,000 bomb load.

As *Phil Sea* steamed back to Korean waters with VADM Clark embarked, the admiral decided to go to Seoul and personally plead the Navy's case. He soon learned that concern over possible MiG interference might scrub the Suiho mission. Additionally, the Navy's contribution had been whittled down to 20 ADs. Com7thFlt personally appealed for the Navy to hit Suiho, not with 20 ADs, but with the 36 he had originally offered. "We ought to send

Philippine Sea with Air Group 11 embarked is moored to Piedmont Pier at Yokosuka, Japan, during her first combat deployment to Korea. During four Korean deployments the new carrier quickly became a veteran while operating with CVG-11, -2 and -9 between 1950 and '53.

as heavy a strike as possible," Clark insisted, "and really clobber that dam." Jocko's persistence helped carry the day.

Round-the-clock planning for the Suiho mission proceeded apace, under the direction of the strike leader, CDR A.L. Downing, CAG-2 in *Boxer*. The pilots who would fly the mission digested the intelligence data and labored under no illusions as to what lay ahead. It would be rough but a welcome change from the drudgery of "working on the railroads." *Philippine Sea* and *Bon Homme Richard* (CV-31) arrived on the scene 23 June joining *Boxer* and *Princeton* (CV-37). For the first time in 18 months, four fleet carriers were operating together off the Korean coast.

At 1400 23 June 1952, the carriers commenced launching the biggest strike of the war at the time: 35 Skyraiders from *Boxer's* VA-65, *Princeton's* VA-195, and *Philippine Sea's* VA-115. The latter, under CDR C.H. Carr, were to attack the hitherto untouched hydroelectric plants. Thirty-one of the ADs hauled a pair of 2,000-pounders and one 1,000-pounder. The other four each carried two 2,000-pounders and one "survival bomb" containing survival gear if anyone was shot down. In addition, 35 F9Fs flew cover: *Boxer's* VF-24, *Princeton's* VF-191 and *Philippine Sea's* VF-112, the latter led by CDR James V. Rowney. Two dozen of the Panthers carried two 250-lb general purpose (GP) bombs, and full ammunition load. Providing top cover over "MiG Alley" were 84 USAF North American F-86 Sabres.

Taking the enemy completely by surprise, the flak-suppression F9Fs led the way while the ADs reversed course and commenced their runs. With the Suiho powerhouse providing an excellent aiming point (a building 80' x 500'), the Navy strike delivered more than 85 tons of bombs in less than two minutes, attacking the powerhouse and the nearby transformer yard and penstocks. They cleared the area with only five planes hit by antiaircraft fire, and all but one returned to their carriers. The exception was an AD-4 from VA-115. The pilot, LTJG M.K. Lake, managed a wheels-up landing at Kimpo airfield near Seoul. Hard on the heels of the carrier strike, 124 Republic F-84G Thunderjets dished out more punishment to the enemy.

The Suiho strike, one of many aimed at the North Korean power complexes that day, was executed like a textbook hop. Although only one pre-strike briefing had been held, the mission went off "as though we had been doing it for years." Post-strike photography, VADM Clark declared, "showed no misses." The powerhouse, in particular, had been hard-hit. As Art Downing stated, it "looked like a volcano erupting." The raid paralyzed not only Pyongyang, the enemy capital, but factories on both sides of the Yalu River; it disrupted the power system of North Korea and Manchuria and forced the relocation of antiaircraft guns defending other key targets. More importantly, the strike implanted serious concern in the minds of the enemy, who lost no time in denouncing the "sneak attacks" on a "project of peaceful construction devoid of all military significance," as to what targets would be next.

For the remainder of *Phil Sea's* second Korean deployment, her planes hammered at hydroelectric complexes and industrial installations, in addition to carrying out limited rail interdiction and destruction of truck shelters. Homeward bound 12 July, the ship reached San Diego 8 August, where, soon thereafter, CAPT Paul H. Ramsey relieved CAPT Smith as CO.

Following limited availability and local operations off Southern California, *Philippine Sea*, reclassified as an attack aircraft carrier, CVA-47, 1 October 1952, returned to the Far East.

Her deck spotted for launch, the fighting Phil Sea prepares to disembark CVG-11 13 March 1951 as she heads for Yokosuka where she will pick up CVG-2 and return to Korea for three more months of combat operations.

She sailed 15 December with Air Group Nine (VF-91, -93 and -94, VA-95, detachments from VC-3, -11, -35 and -61 and a unit of HU-1) embarked. However, damage to one screw forced emergency repairs at Pearl Harbor that delayed the ship's arrival in Yokosuka almost a month. Relieving sister ship *Essex* (CVA-9), *Phil Sea* and her men soon returned to the joyless work of attempting to sever North Korean supply and transportation arteries. CVG-9 launched its first strikes from CVA-47's deck 31 January 1953. She performed interdiction and CAS duties into the spring.

Armistice talks between UN and communist representatives had resumed 26 April after being recessed for 199 days. As the tempo of the war quickened, heavy and bitter fighting developed all along the previously static front lines, as the communists attempted to regain lost ground prior to a negotiated peace. For TF-77 the tempo was likewise hectic, as its carriers launched sorties in poor weather to support the ground troops. With each day, records (tons of bombs and rockets delivered on targets, total number of days at sea, number of sorties flown) fell by the wayside. *Philippine Sea, Boxer Princeton* and *Lake Champlain* (CVA-39) conducted round-the-clock ops 14 and 15 June as TF-77 provided frontline support for the First ROK Corps in its bloody battle to regain "Anchor Hill." For a period of three days during this time, *Phil Sea* suffered engineering problems that forced the use of three screws, and sometimes two. Effecting repairs at sea, the carrier remained on the line, meeting her commitments.

On 27 July 1953 (ironically the day upon which CVG-9 was to rotate home) the armistice stilled the guns in Korea, but not before *Philippine Sea* had launched 49 sorties prior to the truce. During CVA-47's last deployment of the war CVG-9 had flown 7,243 sorties, logged 16,841.7 hours of flight time and 7,704 traps. *Phil Sea's* planes had delivered 8,941,030 lbs of bombs and fired some 385,989 rounds of .50 cal and 618,897 rounds of 20mm. *Philippine Sea* soon sailed for home and reached Alameda 14 August, where she off-loaded her air group. Proceeding to North Island the next day, the ship soon staged another change of command, as CAPT William S. Harris relieved CAPT Ramsey, whose cigar,

Change of command with Captain Waller.

dungaree cap and ready smile had become enduring symbols to his crew. As August drew to a close, the carrier entered drydock at Hunter's Point for overhaul.

Philippine Sea began training off the coast of Southern California 9 January 1954, operating out of San Diego and logged her 60,000th arrested landing. After conducting CarQuals for the pilots of Air Group Five (VF-51, -53 and -54, VF-92 and detachments from VC-35, -11, -3), the ship sailed for the Far East 12 March. The attack carrier reached Pearl Harbor a week later and, after her operational readiness inspection (ORI) sailed for WestPac 3 April.

After conducting task group operations out of the Philippines into late June, CVA-47 sailed for Hong Kong, arriving the 25th for a three day visit. Returning to Manila briefly, the carrier departed for Yokosuka, arriving 2 July for a two-week in-port period. She sailed to take part in routine training operations 16 July. However, an international incident interrupted the routine.

The morning of 22 July 1954, an Air Cathay airliner was proceeding at 9,000 feet on a routine flight from Bangkok to Hong Kong. Steering, clear of Red Chinese Hainan Island, the airliner, her nationality plainly indicated by a 3x5 foot British flag painted on the tail, was 50 miles southeast of Hainan when two Lavochkin LA-7s attacked her. Cannon and machine gun fire from the Chinese fighters set an engine ablaze and punctured a fuel tank. While pilot Philip Blown took evasive action, the two communist fighters took turns riddling the fuselage as their victim slanted toward the water. Blown, a veteran of the Royal Australian Air Force, declared that the attacking pi-

Bitter Korean winters hampered CVG-11 operations and made life miserable for flight deck crews. F9F jet exhaust is used to melt snow and ice.

Ordnance crews build up bombs for next strike.

HU-1's HO3S-1s performed faithful plane guard and logistics duties for Phil Sea from 1950 to 1954.

Above: Quick action by Phil Sea's flight deck crew prevented disaster when F4U-4B caught fire in the pack during 1950 deployment. Right: On loan to ATG-1 for Valley Forge (CV-45) deployment, VF-111 F9F-2B flown by LTJG Robert A. Guyer drops 250-lb bombs near Kowon 23 May 1952. VF-111 first flew combat in Korea in 1950 from CV-47.

lots "... knew what they were doing. They shot us down with the intention of killing us." Six Americans had been among the 18 passengers on board, including a family of five. Of these, Leonard Parish and his two little boys died.

At that time *Philippine Sea*, flagship for ComCarDiv 3, RADM Harry D. Felt, was off the coast of French Indochina, in the waters south of the Paracel Islands, in company with *Hornet* (CVA-12), which had VADM William K. Phillips (ComFirstFlt) embarked. VADM Phillips received a dispatch from NS Sangley Point, R.P., telling of a British commercial airliner in distress and losing altitude southeast of Hainan Island. Phillips immediately directed RADM Felt to conduct a search.

The first launch of the day was canceled and the flight schedule was altered to develop a search plan and brief flight leaders. Knowing that the probable course of the Air Cathay flight was near communist territory, Felt instructed his pilots to not approach land closer than 15 miles. As planning proceeded, the task group steered toward Hainan while two destroyers, operating independently north of the task group, were sent in the direction of the airliner's projected track.

At 0925 *Philippine Sea* launched a jet combat air patrol (CAP), a jet rescue! air patrol (ResCAP), ASW "Gator" aircraft for communication relay, and a search flight of AD-4s. Less than an hour later, at 1030, the force picked up a radio broadcast originating in Hong Kong that gave the last believed position of the missing plane, plus word that a dinghy had been sighted. At 1044 *Hornet* launched a jet ResCAP, a CAP and 10 Skyraiders to take part in the search. Planes from the two carriers arrived in the vicinity of the crash 10 minutes before noon and at 1200 *Hornet* ADs reported a USAF Grumman SA-16A Albatross rescue aircraft from Clark Field "engaged in rescue operations three miles south of Tachao Tho Island, covered by British and French aircraft." The *Hornet* pilots further reported seeing a survivor being picked up from a life raft, and a smoke flare. At 1639 VADM Phillips ordered the search operations suspended after receiving a dispatch from Commander, Naval Forces, Philippines. The task group retired southward having flown 42 search and 64 CAP sorties.

A resumption of the search for survivors soon followed. At 0234 on 25 July the task group received a dispatch from CNO to CinCPacFlt directing ComFirstFlt to continue search and rescue operations for "possible remaining survivors." Within a quarter of an hour the task group was proceeding northward; by 0800 the ships were operating 200 miles south-southeast of Hainan. An hour later, air group and squadron commanders were briefed to: (1) "search thoroughly the area of the crash and along the line of predicted drift northeast of the site." (2) that locating rafts, debris and/or survivors were the primary objects of the search, (3) that small offshore islands were to be carefully inspected, with attention paid to "populated areas where a white man might be hidden, with similar searches to be conducted of junks and sampans." Lastly, pilots were instructed to "not use guns unless attacked or unless aircraft make threatening moves ..."

While the destroyers *Rowe* (DD-564) and *Hunt* (DD-674) operated on a rescue and watchdog station 18 miles east of Tachao Tao, the carriers launched aircraft: a ResCAP of F9F-6s east of Tai Chow Island, an ASW patrol and search patrol of ADs and a low-altitude search and escort CAP of Skyraiders and Corsairs. Air ops continued for nearly 6-1/2 hours, until secured for the day at 1729 as the task group stood out for the night beyond range of shore-based air. The aviators had flown 40 search and 52 CAP/ResCAP sorties.

The pace of operations quickened on the 26th. At 0900 the carriers, steaming into the wind, began launching aircraft. CVG-5's 16 planes were led by CAG-5, CDR George C. "Duke" Duncan, flying a Skyraider.

At about 1010 a pair of Chinese LA-7s attacked CAG's division at 5,000 feet, making a "sloppy, flat side run" from seaward some 15 miles off the east coast of Hainan. Duncan's division countered by turning and diving slightly so that the LA-7s' fire passed overhead. VF-54s, AD-4s and VC-3's F4U-5Ns entered the fray with abandon in what would soon be known as the "Hainan Turkey Shoot." Although vexed by cannon malfunctions (13 of 44 20mm guns in the ADs did not fire), the Americans splashed both communist fighters beyond the 12-mile limit. A Chinese gunboat, escorting two Polish flag merchantmen nearby, opened fire on the carrier aircraft but scored no hits. *Philippine Sea's* pilots showed "admirable restraint" as RADM Felt directed his men to withdraw and not to fire. In the post-mortems of the morning's fray, LT Roy M. Tatham and ENS Richard R. Crooks of VF-54 received credit for shooting down one LA-7. LCDR Paul Wahlstrom (XO of VF-54) and LTJGs Richard S. Ribble, John L. Damian and John M. Rochford shared credit for the second Lavochkin with LCDR E.B. Salsig of VC-3.

After the task group stood to the southward for the night, it conducted further search operations the following day - without result. Ultimately, on orders from CNO, VADM Phillips terminated operations 29 July.

Philippine Sea returned to Manila two days later where RADM R.W. Ruble relieved RADM Felt as ComCarDiv 3. Additionally, on 24 August, the ship welcomed a new CO when CAPT Herman L. Ray relieved CAPT Harris. Outside of visits to Yokosuka and Hong Kong the carrier operated in the Philippine-Formosa area until 27 October 1954.

Returning via *Yokosuka* CVA-47 stopped briefly at Pearl Harbor before reaching San Diego 19 November. Late in the deployment *Phil Sea* served as a movie prop, appearing in the opening moments of the memorable Warner Brothers' film, *Mister Roberts*, helping perpetuate her showboat nickname.

Standing down from her eventful deployment during November and December, *Philippine Sea* resumed training in January 1955, and over the next two months prepared for her fifth cruise to the Orient. With Air Task Group Two embarked (VF-123, -143 and VA-55, plus the usual dets except VC-3), the carrier sailed for Hawaiian waters 1 April. After her ORI off of Pearl Harbor she arrived at Yokosuka 2 May.

Following a five-day in-port period at Yokosuka, CVA-47 embarked upon extensive flight operations and individual ship exercises (ISE) into the summer months. Interspersing her work with liberty visits to Hong Kong and Keelung, Formosa, *Phil Sea* began work with Nationalist Chinese units off the coast of Formosa. During this period, in July 1955, the carrier logged her 70,000th arrested landing, when LTJG Walter G. Offerman of VF-143 trapped in his F9F-6 Cougar.

The next change of command occurred in August when CAPT Elwin L. Farrington relieved CAPT Ray the 13th. Late that month RADM Ira E. Hobbs, who had commanded *Philippine Sea* during part of her Korean War service, came on board and broke his flag as ComCarDiv 3, and concurrently assumed command of TF-77. The ship spent the remainder of her cruise operating with TF-77 and carrying out ISEs, eventually departing Yokosuka on Armistice Day. She reached San Diego 23 November 1955.

With a new generation of attack carriers soon to join the fleet, *Philippine Sea* was now groomed for a new role as an antisubmarine warfare support carrier. She had been reclassified CVS-47 on 15 November and now would operate twin-engine Grumman S2F-1 Trackers and Sikorsky HSS-1 Seabats.

Departing San Diego 6 February 1956, *Phil Sea* shifted to San Francisco where she remained into June under overhaul. Long Beach became her new homeport that month and she operated between the West Coast and Hawaii for the rest of the year. During a July trip to Hawaii with Guided Missile Group One embarked for a homeport change to Barbers Point, the carrier served as the stage for the combat scenes of *Wings of Eagles*. CVS-47 received a new skipper in September when CAPT George S. James Jr. relieved CAPT Farrington.

Standing out of San Diego 5 January 1957, CVS-47 set course once again for Hawaii. After operating out of Pearl Harbor through March, she deployed to the Seventh Fleet. Upon arrival at Yokosuka 8 April the carrier spent the next four months operating the "Stoofs" of VS-37 and Seabats of HS-2. Departing the Far East 24 July, *Philippine Sea* returned to San Diego 6 August. Later that day she shifted to Long Beach where she spent the next month. The remainder of the year was devoted to local ops - qualifying and refresher day and night training for VS-21, -23 and -37 and day landings by helos from HS-2, -4 and -6, interspersed with a "hunter-killer" exercise. On 21 September 1957 CAPT Magruder H. Tuttle relieved CAPT James as CO.

Highlighting the fall was the ship's part in a major search operation. Indeed, the largest in recent memory, involving more than 29 aircraft and 14 ships.

On the morning of 8 November 1957, Pan American Airways (PAA) flight 944 took off from San Francisco.

The Boeing Stratocruiser named *Romance of the Skies* was bound for Honolulu with 36 passengers and a crew of eight on board. It passed Ocean Station "November," the point of no return between the West Coast and Hawaii, early that evening and made a routine report. When it failed to arrive as scheduled, vanishing without any hint of trouble, an intensive search immediately commenced.

On 9 November Commander, Naval Air Force, PacFlt, directed ComCarDiv 17 (RADM Thomas A. Ahroon), in *Philippine Sea*, to embark VS-21 and HS-6 and sail for Ocean Station November. CAPT Tuttle, utilizing the local TV and radio stations, immediately recalled all officers and men from leave and liberty. Aided in preparations for sea by volunteers from *Boxer*, CVS-47 sailed at 2330 with nearly 75% of her complement on board. HS-6's 10 HSS-1s, under CDR Ernest C. Harris Jr., landed on board just prior to departure. Joined by the destroyers *John R. Craig* (DD-885) and *Duncan* (DDR-874), *Philippine Sea* proceeded toward the last known position of *Romance of the Skies*, landing 13 S2Fs of VS-21 (led by CDR Leo Meacher), on the morning of the 10th.

Phil Sea launched four Trackers to commence the search at 1600 on the 11th. Early the following morning, the ship, joined by two additional destroyers, *Epperson* (DDE-719) and *Renshaw* (DDE-449), launched her second search, four Trackers and four Seabats. By the time CVS-47 secured from flight operations on the 13th, her aircraft had searched some 64,000 square miles of ocean, 12 hours a day.

At 0645 14 November, *Philippine Sea* commenced launch of four S2Fs and four HSS-1s. A little under an hour later, at 0735, ADC F.T. Kingsley, radar operator in the S2F flown by LCDR Paul G. Cowan and LTJG Leo J. Gaffrey, picked up a "small and intermittent" contact.

Captain Macgruder H. Tuttle, USN.

LCDR Cowan soon sighted something in the water and took the S2F down to investigate. Orbiting the object twice, he determined it to be a piece of wreckage from the lost plane. About the same time another S2F, flown by LTJGs Earl E. Carlovsky and John N. Stanley, sighted another piece of wreckage and a body. While Cowan circled to maintain visual contact, Carlovsky climbed to radio the carrier.

RADM Ahroon, apprised of the find, directed all surface units to proceed to the area at their best speed. Summoned to the scene, the other two airborne S2Fs joined in the search, marking the debris with smoke bombs and continuing to look for survivors. Epperson arrived first and lowered boats to pick up debris and the first victim. *Phil Sea*, preceded by her helicopters, arrived at 1140 and commenced additional searches.

All ships lowered boats and, assisted by the hovering helos, carried out the grim task of recovering victims and debris from a 33-square mile area, working ceaselessly until darkness. The shoeless, life-jacketed victims bore mute testimony to the fact that a ditching had perhaps been attempted. Eventually joined by USCGC *Minnetonka* (WPG-67), the effort recovered 17 bodies, numerous packets of mail and small debris. At first light the following day, the group resumed the search, recovering two more bodies before 1000. Only, additional debris turned up thereafter, with no sign of the other 25 people on board the ill-fated *Stratocruiser*. During the two days of recovery operations *Phil Sea's* Trackers swept an additional 20,000 square miles without success. Ultimately, upon RADM Ahroon's recommendation, Commander, Hawaiian Sea Frontier, terminated search operations at 1800 on the 15th. The ASW carrier returned to Long Beach three days later.

Philippine Sea began her last year of commissioned service operating out of Long Beach, sailing on her final WestPac deployment 13 January 1958 with VS-21 and HS-6 embarked. Proceeding via Pearl Harbor, the ship reached Subic Bay 31 January. She operated out of Subic through late February, swinging through the waters of Okinawa's Buckner Bay and back to the Philippines before reaching Yokosuka 5 April for a five-day stay. Returning to Subic, *Phil Sea* logged her 82,000th arrested landing 24 April when LTJG Leo Gaffrey brought his Tracker aboard. The carrier then visited Singapore, engaging in Exercise Oceanlink 1-13 May. A multilateral SEATO (Southeast Asia Treaty Organization) operation, it included the British carrier HMS *Bulwark* and the Australian carrier HMAS *Melbourne*. CVS-47 conducted "cross-decking" ops with both commonwealth carriers.

Departing Yokosuka 2 July, *Philippine Sea* arrived at San Diego the 15th, moving to Long Beach the following day. She returned to San Diego briefly to offload her last embarked aviation units, VS-21 and HS-6, before sailing back to Long Beach on the 25th. On 14 August 1958 *Phil Sea* was ordered to report to Commander, Pacific Reserve Fleet for phase "bravo" inactivation, which occurred the 22nd. That same day CAPT Tuttle turned over command to his XO, CDR James G. Hedrick. During her active career the proud carrier had logged a total of 82,813 landings and 33,575 catapult launches.

Only 12 years old, *Philippine Sea* was placed out of commission, in reserve, 22 December 1958 and berthed at the Long Beach Naval Shipyard. Inactivated without an overhaul, she was deemed to have "no potential for operating high-performance aircraft without complete modernization." By the same token, because of her size, it was thought that she could only "achieve restricted capability after modernization." She was accordingly designated as an "auxiliary aircraft carrier transport," AVT-11, effective 15 May 1959, along with three of her sisters, *Franklin* (AVT-8), *Bunker Hill* (AVT-9) and *Leyte* (AVT-10).

A decade later the Navy again looked at *Philippine Sea*. By that point, however, she was an "unimproved World War II axial deck aircraft carrier." To "activate, repair and modernize the ship to fulfill the mission of an anti-submarine warfare support carrier would be an unprofitable expenditure of limited resources." Accordingly, the president of the Board of Inspection and Survey found *Philippine Sea* "unfit for further naval service," and recommended that she be stricken from the Naval Vessel Register. Deemed "not essential to the defense of the United States," *Philippine Sea* was stricken 1 December 1969 and sold for scrap 23 March 1971 to Zidell Explorations, Inc., of Portland, Oregon.

The name *Philippine Sea* and the deeds of her men, however, have not been forgotten. On 9 June 1986, Secretary of the Navy John F. Lehman Jr., mindful of not only the significance of the 1944 battle but of the accomplishments of *Phil Sea*, assigned the name to a Ticonderoga-class (CG-47) guided missile cruiser that had been laid down at Bath Iron Works 8 May 1986. Launched 12 July 1987, the new *Philippine Sea* (CG-58) is to be delivered to the Navy early in 1989. The crew of this new warship should derive considerable pride from the accomplishments of her illustrious predecessor and crews who served their country so well.

Acknowledgments

CAPT George C. Duncan, USN (Ret)
LTJG Ted Korsgren, USNR (Ret)
ETCM Allan G. LeBaron, USN (Ret)
CDR John M. Rochford, USN (Ret)
Roland H. Baker Jr.
PHCM David B. Benton, USN (Ret)

Flight deck crew respots the deck 15 May 53 during CVA-47's final Korean combat tour. CVG-9 was embarked for final months of the war which ended 27 July 1953 but brought the highest intensity carrier strikes in its history.

Left: Philippine Sea during refueling operations with Chemung (AO-30) and Airborn (D-631) 26 April 1954. Below: VF-54 AD-4 comes aboard during July 1954 operations off Hainan. Below Center: Jubilant VF-54 pilots involved in shootdown of two Chinese LA-7 fighters during the "Hainan Incident" 25 July 1954. (seated from left) ENS J.J. Zardus and LTJG J.M. Rochford (standing) LTJGs R.S. Ribble, J.L. Damian and LCDRs W.H. Alexander, P.J. Wahlstrom. Bottom: LT Roy M. Tatham (left) and CAG-5 CDR George C. Duncan (center) confer with VF-54 skipper CDR Christian Fink.

THE DEPLOYMENTS OF USS *PHILIPPINE SEA* (CV/CVA/CVS-47)

Shakedown	15 Oct-20 Nov 46/27 Mar-5 May 1947	
CVG-20 (CVAG-9)	Carribbean	
VF-20 (VF-9A	F8F-1/F6F-5P	20-F-XX
VBF-20 (VF-10A)	F8F-1	20-BF-XX
VB-20 (VA-9A)	SB2C-5	20-B-XX
VT-20 (VA-10A)	TBM-3E	20-T-XX
(CVG-20 became CVAG-9 15 Nov 46)		

1. 9 Feb-26 Jun 48
CVAG-9 Mediterranean

VF-9A	F8F-1/F6F-5P	PS 100
VF-10A	F8F-1/F6F-5P	PS 200
VA-9A	SB2C-5	PS 300
VA-10A	TBM-3E/Q	PS 400
VCN-2 Team 4	F6F-5N	LA 120
HU-2 Det	HO3S-1	

2. 4 Jan-31 May 49
CVG-7 Mediterranean

VF-71	F8F-1/F6F-5P	L 100
VF-72	F8F-1	L 200
VF-73	F8F-1	L 300
VA-74	F4U-4	L 400
VC-4 Det	F6F-5N	NA 50
HU-2 Det	HO3S-1	UR XX

3. 24 Jul 50-26 Mar 51
CVG-11 Korea

VF-111	F9F-2	V 100
VF-112	F9F-2	V 200
VF-113	F4U-4B	V 300
VF-114	F4U-4B	V 400
VA-115	AD-4/-Q	V 500
VC-3 Det	F4U-5N/AD-4N	NP XX
VC-11 Det	AD-4W	ND XX
VC-61 Det	F4U-4P	PP XX
HU-1 Det 3	HO3S-1	UP20

(3A) 28 Mar-9 Jun 51
CVG-2 Korea (CVG-11 crossdecked with CVG-2 from CV-45)

VF-64	F4U-4	M 100
VF-63	F4U-4	M 200

VF-24	F4U-4	M 400
VA-65	AD-2/Q/4	M 500
VC-3 Det	F4U-5N	NP 10
VC-11 Det	AD-4W	ND XX
VC-35 Det 4	AD-4N	NR 80
VC-61 Det	F4U-4P	PP XX
HU-1 Det	HO3S-1	UP 20

4. 31 Dec 51-8 Aug 52
CVG-11 Korea

VF-112	F9F-2	V 200
VF-113	F4U-4	V 300
VF-114	F4U-4	V 400
VA-115	AD-4	V 500
VC-3 Unit C	F4U-5N/NL	NP 10
VC-11 Unit C	AD-4W	ND 20
VC-35 Unit C	AD-4NL/Q/-2Q	NR 30
VC-61 Unit C	F2H-2P/F9F-2P	PP 70/90
HU-1 Unit	HO3S-1	UP 20

5. 15 Dec 52-14 Aug 53
CVG-9 Korea

VF-91	F9F-2	N 100
VF-93	F9F-2	N 300
VF-94	F4U-4	N 400

Fighting Squadron 9-A (VF-9A). USS Philippine Sea (CV47). April-May 1947.

VA-95	AD-4/NA/L	N 500
VC-3 Unit M	F4U-FN	NP 1
VC-11 Unit M	AD-4W	ND 90
VC-35 Unit M	AD-4N	NR XX
VC-61 Unit M	F9F-5P	PP 20
HU-1 Unit	HO3S-1	UP XX

6. 12 Mar-19 Nov 54
CVG-5 WESTPAC

VF-51	F9F-6	S 100
VF-92	F9F-2	N 200
VF-53	F9F-2	S 300
*VF-54	AD-4/B/L	S 400
VC-3 Det B	F4U-5N	NP 10
VC-11 Unit B	AD-4W	ND XX
VC-35 Unit B	AD-4NL	NR XX
VC-61 Unit B	F9F-6P	PP XX
HU-1 Unit 16	HO3S-1/HUP-2	UP 30

*Operated ADs as a VF Squadron

7. 1 Apr-23 Nov 55
ATG-2 WESTPAC

VF-143	F9F-6	A 100
VF-123	F9F-2	D 300
VA-55	AD-6	S 500
C-11 Det I	AD-4W	ND 40
VC-35 Det I	AD-5N	NR 90
VC-61 Det I	F9F-5P	PP 20
HU-1 Unit 16	HUP-2	UP 10

8. 5 Jan-6 Aug 57
WESTPAC

VS-37	S2F-1/2	SU 1
HS-2	HSS-1	SK 1

9. 13 Jan-15 Jul 58
WESTPAC

VS-21	S2F-1/2	YA 1
HS-6	HSS-1	UB 1

USS PHILIPPINE SEA
SPECIAL STORIES

First Korean Cruise Philippine Sea Heroes
by CTC Edward E. Nugent, USN (Ret)

During my years at the National Museum of Naval Aviation as a volunteer tour guide and occasional writer I have had the honor of meeting and often getting to know true national heroes. Men like the late George Gay, Joe Foss, Flying Tiger Ace Tex Hill, Midway hero Richard Best and several of the astronauts. I must say, however, that my memories of Philippine Sea heroes fit very well for me into this select group. I believe all former men of CV-47 and her air groups should remember and be proud to have served with heroes not so well known but who made their mark by very distinguishing service.

I remember the day early in the war when an AD Skyraider flown by Ensign Darrell Knight returned with a fragmentation bomb hanging from his port wing. When the plane hit the deck the bomb dropped off and went skidding down the deck, the sparks flew and no one knew what would happen. AB1 Tieranzzano with Airman Jack Johnson and AB3 M.H. Cook ran out and picked up the 250 lb. bomb and threw it over the side. Most Abs will remember "Terry" Tieranzzano broke all the rules by calling everyone by their first name, but no one had more respect as a Navy man.

I was in the catapult crew and we were often at what was called "Condition 10." A plane, usually the F4U as I recall, would be hooked up to the Cat and be turned up so it could be shot off quickly. I remember air group commander, Commander Vogel, on an occasion came out to the plane and talked to some including this "green kid." Later I saw him on the hanger deck and how pleased I was that he called me by name when he returned my salute. I was wearing my green flight deck sweater so he wasn't reading my name from my shirt. Soon after that in September 1950, he was shot down. I have heard he bailed out but his chute only streamed above him. I remember I didn't want my shipmates in the catapult machine room berthing space see me cry, but now push-

USS Philippine Sea.

USS Philippine Sea at Yokusulea, Japan. June 1958.

S2F Tracker plane on USS Philippine Sea.

ing age 70, I "tear up" every time I think of him. A fine man who was not pompous or arrogant but spoke to a young airman with respect. His service in the air and in command is what many may remember, but I remember a family man who died too young.

Then of course I remember the helo pilot, Chief Duane W. Thorin. I am sure many of the crew felt the pride I did of an AP flying from our ship. He was later shot down and taken prisoner, escaped and recaptured as I recall. He retired as lieutenant but to me he will always be the Chief that made rescues and flew the admiral around.

There were many others, like Lieutenant Anthony Modica, the aircraft service officer. Not only did he keep the planes flying but it was he who devised the "still" system of heating the gasoline so they could make napalm in sub-zero weather. Yet when he was put in for the Bronze Star his comment was that his men made him look good. Yes, to me these were all heroes whether they were shot at or not. I've told my kids, if I had known I was living through history I would have kept better notes.

A White Hat

To borrow a few words from Admiral Daniel Gallery, a White Hat is a crafty individual that bears watching at all times. With that in mind here is a tale from the early 50s that proves it to be so:

Back, way back in the days when North American Bluejackets still wore liberty uniforms ashore on liberty and you could still wear a uniform south of the border to Tiajuana, a young, fairly young and dumb, bluejacket did just that. He had never been to "TJ" but he had heard enough that he wanted to go see for himself, again, he was alone and often preferred it that way. He'd been in the Merchant Marine for eight years and had often wandered about in foreign lands so there was nothing particularly frightening or so it seemed to him. He boarded a bus in San Diego and off he went.

"TJ" or "TeeJay" as Tiajuana is known was a wide open town in the early 50s. Anything and everything could and would be found there, foreign visitors were catered to, indulged and encouraged. It was a time when many high school kids from Southern California, mainly from Los Angeles, could go and explore life in a way they couldn't in their own (they'd get locked up for it at home)!

Our enterprising young bluejacket got off the bus at the border and proceeded by cab into the main part of town. Many, many stalls of leather crafted items were on display along with the required huaraches made of leather and auto tire soles, silver jewelry (some very nicely made and extremely reasonable), and taco stands. Lots and lots of taco stands on the sidewalks and in the streets; one couldn't avoid them. Oh yeah, there were also the street runners who wanted you to buy French post cards or pornographic cartoon books that utilized the North American comic strip heroes, small to high potency drugs and all of that there.

Well, I wasn't all that interested in that but had worked up a sweat and a thirst so off to the main drag and the gin joints. After hitting a few, found out they were worse than Panama, and that's bad! Started to get sleepy, so headed back to the border and "DAGO." Somehow, all alone I lost my crackerjack white hat. Oooopppppsss! I'm in trouble, Babe. May sound stupid now, but after a few drinks back then, still reeling from ROCKS & SHOALS, anything that could get you in trouble could make your bowels turn to ice. Out of uniform? Not a major issue but, first, have to get out of town and back to the ship. Easy, got off the bus and headed south, didn't know where I was going but I had evaded the Shore Patrol so at least I was on my way. Whoa!! What's this ahead? Some kind of a car wrecking yard. Minor barbed wire fence, a quick glance around, up and over and I was in. Looked around a bit and saw just what the Dr. ordered, a steering wheel, latched on to that baby and was on my way, I thought. "Hey Mac!" ever hear those sounds and responded to them like they were your long lost buddies (or not), or you hear it with that sound that says you just stepped into it big, as I turned I spotted two of San Diego's finest getting out of a plainclothes car.

There was not a doubt in my military mind that I hadn't stepped into it big time, I mean face it, even as drunk as I was, two cops steppin' out of an undercover car at two, three o'clock in the morning and speaking to me like we had been introduced gave me bad feelings. Still, duty calls and I sauntered over, casual like. "What's going on, Man? The questions from both sides had a nice ring to them on the dark deserted streets. Most of you know the drill, ID produced, walked to their car, put in the back while I answered questions. The night most have been long and boring because they said give us your story and I did. Until they nabbed me my plan had been to make it back to the ship via the Strand. Long before the bridge, anyway, make it back and present myself to the OOD with steering wheel in hand, admit I'd had an accident, but the car was a junker anyway and all that was left was the wheel and, oh yeah, I lost my white hat too. They looked at each other and laughed themselves silly, till one of them asked me if I could pull it off. "No doubt in my military mind, Sir"

Short story, they drove me over the Silver Strand, got permission to drive me to the USS *Philippine Sea*. They marched me smartly up the forward brow to hear me give my spiel to the OOD. He asked the two San Diego officers if charges where pending. "No, what are your plans for him sir?" He looked confused, asked me if I was all right, after my affirmative, and told me to go hit my rack. I had had enough action for the evening. The two cops? All I could hear was their laughter going down the gangway. Conclusion? The Admiral stated it best "A White Hat is a crafty individual that bears watching at all times."

Sailor Story (True - I was There)
by H. Flint Ranney, LTJG, USN

The *Philippine Sea* was to be decommissioned in December of 1958. During the final WestPac cruise, the captain and executive officer decided to have a full-power run to see if the old girl could still hit 32 knots.

The engineers lit off all eight boilers, the bridge signaled all-ahead flank, the navigator picked a course that would allow us to steam in a straight line for many miles, and we all watched the speed indicator creep up to 30.5 knots, where it stayed.

The captain, exec, operations officer, and chief engineer huddled on the bridge and decided that the stern was dipping down too far and we needed more weight at the bow to even up the keel and allow the ship to go just a little faster. This decision was announced over the PA system: "All hands not actually on watch report to the bow." Hundreds of crewmen crowded up and stood around waiting to find out why they were there.

The speed indicator was stuck at 30.5 knots. The XO said, "Let's line up the airplanes on the flight deck and run up their engines to help pull us through the water faster!" The Air Department found about 20 S2Fs (twin-engine "hunter-killer" planes), tied them down securely, and told the pilots to advance their throttles to full speed. After about 10 minutes

(Courtesy of H. Flint Ranney.)

the air officer began to complain to the bridge that the aircraft engines would overheat and be damaged if this maneuver continued, so the operation was closed down and the crew was allowed to leave the bow area; 30.5 knots was the best the ship could do.

The Ship
by Edgar Siewert

It was dusk when we arrived at the dock in the naval yard. A bus that had picked us up at North Station in Boston where we left the train that brought us from Great Lakes Training Station. I got out of the bus saying, "Where's the ship?"

The petty officer in charge said, "You're looking at it."

"Where?"

"Right there," he pointed in front of me to a large gray wall.

"I thought we were standing on a street between two large buildings and that was one of them," I said looking to the right and left and sure enough the building curved like a ship and the roof stuck over part of the side like a flight deck. It was an aircraft carrier!

The *Philippine Sea* (CV-47) was a new aircraft carrier that had just been commissioned. We were part of the original crew.

We climbed steps and a gang plank 30 feet over the dock. To the main or hanger deck where we faced the rear of the ship and saluted the national color. Stepped onto the deck and saluting the Office of the Day, OD with, "Request permission to come aboard, Sir."

"Permission granted." He returned the salute, as the OD did every time you came aboard the ship. The petty officer took us to our quarters on the fourth deck below the hanger deck saying, "You will sleep here tonight. The heads (bath rooms) are on the third deck. You'll eat on the second deck. Someone will wake you in the morning for chow and tell you where to go for duty. Pick any bunk that isn't made up. Lights are out at 2200 hours but the red lights stay on all night." These were night lights because with all the lights out you couldn't see anything, and for those on duty they had to see to get around.

We surveyed the compartment, it had bunks four high with 56 of them in all. There were lockers 18 inches square, stacked four high, one for each bunk or sailor. On the top of the lockers were fans with rubber blades, in case the man on the top bunk got his fingers or toes in it in the middle of the night. And they did once in a while which would wake most of us.

There was a ladder (stairs) on the one end for getting into and out of the compartment and a locked hatch below it, where ship's supply was stored. To the left of the hatch were two large 6 foot tall laundry bags, one for whites and one for dark clothes that the whole compartment used. Butt cans were scattered around the compartment in many open spaces for cigarette butts.

I choose a bottom bunk on the opposite end of the compartment from the latter, thinking it would be more quiet. It was, but it was near one of those red lights, that hung about 18 inches above the floor, which bothered me all night. Plus, I didn't have my blankets and felt like I'd freeze with just my pea-coat covering me. The next night I switched to a higher bunk where the red lights didn't shine in my face.

All the air in the compartment was brought in by blowers.

In the winter it was heated and in the summer it was outside temperature. At night you could hear these blowers so for a few nights I had trouble sleeping until I got used to them. The first time I went on leave, after being on ship for sometime, I couldn't sleep because it was too quiet.

The next day we were taken to the electricians main working compartment on the second deck. They told us they had requested 20 electricians and received 20 electrical strikers, which in our case were graduates of electrical school working to be electrical petty officers. Because there were too many strikers they were going to put us in other sections of the engineering department until they could use us. I was assigned to the machinist gang and told to report to number one machine room.

"Where is it?" I asked.

"I don't know but look for it till you find it. You can stay in our quarters until they move you," I was told.

Another man, assigned there also, and I started looking for the number one machine room. We asked everyone but they were all new to the ship too and didn't know. After two days we finally found it, the hatch was outside of the electrical compartment door where we had originally started.

The machinist takes care of the ship's machinery that propel the ship, the steam turbines, shafts, and screws. There is a lot of other jobs they do too, like making water to drink and use in the boilers. All the strikers in this section had been trained as a machinist and knew what they were doing but I was lost.

They gave me a cleaning station, an area I was responsible to clean and keep painted. I was assigned watches (duties) around the clock, in different areas like everyone else.

The worst watch was on the evaporators, which is where the salt water is converted to fresh water for the ship. It was in the bilge of the ship where you could stand or sit on the expanded metal deck about three feet above the very bottom. You had to watch a water column to be sure it didn't lose water and a pressure gauge to be sure it didn't lose pressure. This lasted four hours at a time as all watches did. You couldn't read, write, sleep or do anything but watch those instruments and smoke. Once in a while the roving guard would come around and talk to you. If this didn't drive you stir crazy nothing would. They had a lot of watches like this.

The ship put out a ship's paper the *Philippine Sea Line* once or twice a week and they

USS Philippine Sea in port.

had an article in there about being short cooks and bakers. So I talked to the warrant officer in charge of them about it and they transferred me to the bakery. I didn't have any training there either but might as well learn something I could do outside of the Navy, plus the liberty was better. Out of every two weeks, you were off a total of one week in one to three day passes. When you were on duty you were on for 12 to 36 hours.

This was more liberty than I could afford so I spent a lot of time looking over the ship and on the beach at Quonset Point Naval base.

There was a store room under the bakery for a week's supply of bakery products. Every Thursday the warrant officer, chief baker on duty, and a work party would go to the large storage area to draw the next week's requirements and put them in the bakery store room.

One time when the ship was out to sea by itself, the head baker on duty discovered we didn't have enough raisins for raisin pie. He went to the warrant officer, who had the keys to the large storage area, to see if he could go get some raisins. The warrant officer said, "Supplies are to be drawn on Thursday and you should have done it then."

The baker said," I wasn't on duty and who ever was must have missed them on the menu."

"Well you can't draw them now! That's the rule. But you had better have raisin pie for dinner or you'll be in big trouble."

The baker came back saying, "Go down in our store room and get everything that is left over from other meals." We came back with 21 gallons of apples, 13 gallons of pears, 15 gallons of peaches, 18 gallons of apricots, 13 gallons of grapes, 20 gallons of pineapple, 22 gallons of fruit cocktail, 19 gallons of plums, 17 gallons of cherries and proceeded to dump them all in our mixing tub and mix them up. It looked like fruit cocktail. Then we dumped some cases of raisins we had left over into it and it looked like black s#%!. We turned all this into pie and served it to the crew. Who asked, "What's this?"

"Raisin pie, eat it you'll like it," we said since we got to serve all the pastries.

The warrant officer was so impressed that after that every so often we would do it again to clean up the left over fruit, calling it fruit cocktail pie.

We baked all the bread for the ship which was our biggest job. All the left over bread was turned into bread pudding.

The first 30 days I was in the bakery I couldn't get enough pastries to eat but after that I lost interest in them. But all the crew was your friend and stopped by from watches to see if we had any pastries left, which we always gave them.

After five or six months in the bakery they had some openings in the electrical gang so I asked my chief if I could get transferred back. He said, "No. Since you requested a transfer in, we're not obligated to transfer you back. Besides we need people just like the engineering department."

"Can I talk to the warrant officer about it?" I asked.

"Yes but it wouldn't do any good. You know how mean he is and since we need you, he'll say no. But you can talk to him."

I decided to talk to the warrant officer, what did I have to lose.

"I always wanted to be an electrician when I got in the Navy," the warrant officer said, "but then I got a rating in this field and couldn't afford to change. I hope you make it and if you do, be a good one," he told me as he signed my transfer.

TO ANTARCTICA AND BACK
by Edgar A. Siewert

November 1946 the ship left Quonset Point, Rhode Island for Norfolk, Virginia without any airplanes. On the way out of Narragansett Bay the ship was breaking a solid sheet of ice four to six inches deep.

In Norfolk where the weather was better, we loaded the ship with supplies for Admiral Richard E. Byrd's Operation Highjump to Antarctica. The hanger deck had all kinds of snow removal equipment for our ship and lots of supplies to be transferred to other ships at Antarctica. We loaded the flight deck with six R4Ds or DC3, two light airplanes and two helicopters,

January 2, 1947 the ship was under way from Norfolk, Virginia to the Panama Canal Zone. We arrived in Cristobal, CZ on January 7, where the ship was rigged to go through the canal by stowing equipment that would be in the way. I went on pass here but one day was plenty, not much to do.

January 8, underway for transit through the canal. It was very interesting. There are three locks at each end of it to raise the ship 85 feet to pass through the canal and lower it that amount to the Pacific Ocean. The ship did bang the side and chip some of the concrete on the locks. The flight deck hung over the sides of the locks and damaged some of the electric locomotives, called "mules," that towed the ship through.

The ship had to be rigged for sea again in Panama City so we rated more liberty. Panama City was having its Mardigras with a parade down the main streets and celebrations everywhere. Four of us took a taxi tour of old Panama, the first settlement in the new world. We saw an old ruins, the first keystone bridge, and cave that prisoners were chained in to be drowned at high tide. He took us to a building that look like a hotel surrounded by a six foot brick wall. "What is this," we asked.

"It is a House of Love where you can get girls," was his answer. "You can go in the bar

and have a drink if you would like to look it over or stay. I'll wait for you."

It was all very interesting, or so the big boys said.

Later a shoe shine boy on the street said, "Sailor, I'll give a free shoe shine."

"What's the catch kid?" I asked,

"No catch. It's good for business. People see me giving you a shoe shine they come over cause they know sailors get the best."

That makes sense. "OK give me that free shoe shine." He finished with first one and I put my other shoe up on the box to be shined.

He said, "That shoe will be a dollar and a half. I said a free shoe shine, not shoes." I had to get it shined or it would have looked strange with one so shiny.

We went to a bar where you could get Milwaukee Beer who's slogan was "The beer that made Milwaukee jealous."

The last evening we ended up in an bar down town that had lots of pretty girls and a tattoo artist in the corner fixing up the drunken sailors. We sat down at a table and some young ladies came over to visit with us saying, "Would you fellows like to dance?" So we did. Then they asked, "Would you buy us a drink?" So we did. We drank and danced until we realize we were getting a little tipsy but they were sober so we tried one of their drinks. It was just a cola with no alcohol in it but we were paying for mixed drinks. We wised up, they were working for the establishment, so we dumped them. Sure enough they found some other suckers to prey on.

We watched the tattoo artist and the fools getting them while we were drinking. But we watched too long and got too drunk. The next morning when I awoke I had a bandage on my left, forearm. I carefully pulled a corner of it up to see the sickest mess I'd every seen. Then I pulled it all off and there was a tattoo in red, blue, green and yellow with dried blood intermingled. What a sight, I almost cried. It was some kind of sea serpent that I needed like a hole in my head.

One day in Panama City one of the men came back from shore, about noon with a wrist watch he paid $20 for. He said he had bargained the man down to that, and it looked like it was worth it. About 1800 hours another man came in with the same wrist watch he had talked the seller down $12. At 2200 hours another returned from liberty with the same watch he got for $2, just a better talker.

January 11 the ship hoisted the "Jolly Rogers," the skull and cross bones flag, for the commencing of the Neptune Ceremony, because the ship had crossed the equator. The ceremony, lasted two days. There are two classes of sailors on board a ship: shellbacks, those that have been across the equator, and pollywogs, those that have not. I was a pollywog like two-thirds of the ship and all but one in our gang. The first day we did stupid stuff, dressed goofy, counted all the planks in the flight deck and did anything within reason that a shellback asked us to. Shellbacks were dressed like pirates and were just as mean and tough.

After about a half a day of this foolishness some of us in our gang locked our shellback, Bowen, behind the switchboard in the Intercommunication Room where he couldn't get out. It is six decks below the hanger deck where no one goes unless they have business. Eventually everyone left except the man on duty who let Bowen talk him into a release. Bowen rounded up some other shellbacks and they made life difficult for us to say the least. Thank God we were going to the Antarctica because the ship's captain wouldn't let them shave our heads.

The second day they had all the pollywogs in skivvies, waiting on the hanger deck for our uncertain fate. We were herded by groups, like sheep, onto the forward elevator for a trip to the flight deck to meet Davy Jones and Neptunus Rex, perched upon their thrones. With growing apprehension we approached the judges and noticed with horror the operating tables filled with ailing pollywogs, chains and irons fastened to some others and the various forms of torture the shellback judges were doling out. Then we mounted the steps of a ladder to sit in a chair, that flopped over backward throwing us into a briny pool of salt water four feet deep. Gasping for breath, we scrambled out of the pool to land sprawling on a greased canvas sheet. Trying to recover we were thoroughly greased by several shellbacks with oily swabs, swatting us like painting a post. Then the final torture; we had to run down a long canvas with the shellbacks on both sides wildly swinging shillelaghs at us. We emerged battered, swollen, torn, dirty, but proud shellbacks of the most worthy and honorable nature. They only had one shower in the rear of the ship for possibly 2,000 of us to use and it had ocean salt water in it. Have you ever tried to get clean with salt water when you are oily and greasy?

The next exciting thing to happened was the ship's, helicopter took off on its maiden flight and crashed 75 yards to port side of the ship. The three fellows that were on board were picked up by the motor whale boat and crew.

January 23-We sighted the first iceberg.

January 24-The ship crossed the Antarctica Circle, there was some snow and sleet. Icebergs were everywhere so that night the ship stopped to lay to, didn't steam, just drifted with the ice, so we wouldn't run into one of the bergs.

The icebergs towered as high as 200 feet and the longest I saw measured about 3 miles on radar. The top is usually flat unless it has been worn down by the water. They have a light blue-green color and were everywhere. What you see out of the water is only one third of the berg, it is possible for them to have fingers several miles long under water.

The next day we rendezvoused with the other ships of our fleet: a freighter, icebreaker, destroyer and a submarine. They had sailed through the ice that got as thick as 70 feet in some places. The submarine couldn't handle this so it was serving as a weather station out of the ice pack.

We started off-loading everything we brought down for them, including 30 foot long bamboo poles, four inches in diameter used to mark trails on Antarctica. We transferred some personnel in a boatswains seat and some got a little wet when the line would slack so they would hit the water.

We were in the Bay of Whales where the whales come during the Antarctic summers, there were hundreds of them that would come to top and spout, then disappear. The largest I saw must have been 90 feet long, of course only about four to eight feet of their back ever get out of the water.

There was some nice days when the sun was up for 20 of the 24 hours, it would almost go from sunset to sunrise.

The most important job of the *Philippine Sea* was the launching of the six R4D transports, which took place on the 29th and 30th. They had been waiting for good weather at the carrier and 500 miles away at Little America.

Ski wheel combinations had been installed on the R4Ds, while on board, to take off on wheels and land on skies, after arriving at Little America the wheels were removed.

The ship swung into the wind and cranked up about 30 knots of speed. The first R4D was moved into place and started, then they fastened on a jato bottle on each side of the fuselage behind the wings. At 2215 on the evening of the 29th, the first R4D was launched with Admiral Byrd on board. It was off of the deck in about a 100 feet. It circled the ship until number two was launched, then both flew to Little America, while it was still light. Early the next morning the next two were launched and by 0720 the last pair were on their way.

Unlike the weather conditions during the off loading, flying conditions were ideal. The ceiling at Little America opened in time for the planes to land, but closed in within 30 minutes after the last plane had landed. The *Philippine Sea* then returned to off-loading and refueling the other ships before heading back to Quonset Point, Rhode Island.

On a clear night you can see the Southern Cross which is used to navigate in the southern hemisphere like the North Star in the northern. Also, the water does drain out of the drains clock-wise in the southern hemisphere, thought you wanted to know.

Just outside of the Antarctica circle on our way home I was promoted to fireman first class. Only four more steps to chief petty officer.

During the return trip, the crew had more time to relax and enjoy themselves. Two smokers (boxing matches) were held at that time, as well as many sports and much sunbathing under the sultry tropical sun. This is the first suntan I ever got during the winter months.

The voyage totaling 18,000 miles was finally completed at Quonset Point.

A Sailor's Story
by James L. Wright

It was Sunday and the *Philippine Sea* was rigged for church. We were somewhere in the Mediterranean, Spring of 1947. I was a AMM3/c in Squadron VF10A and I had the duty. The chief sent me topside to do some minor repair on one of our planes, an F8F Bear Cat.

The elevators weren't working so I had to go up through the ladders in the island. I had my toolbox, which weighed about 80 lbs (I weighed in at 130, tops).

Halfway up through the island who do I meet but the admiral with his Marine guard, who yells at me "gang way." I had no place to go on the narrow landing and there I stood, in my work clothes and baseball cap, facing the man higher than God in his spotless dress whites. I didn't know what would be the best thing to do - faint, salute or jump overboard.

Fortunately, the admiral realized what I was about and said, "You have a job to do on the flight deck? Carry on!

His guard, in his immaculate dress blues, glared at me as he tried to pass me without soiling his uniform on my work dungarees.

This happened over 50 years ago and it's as vivid in my mind as if it were yesterday. This skinny 19-year-old kid meeting the admiral.

USS *Philippine Sea* Engineering Department
by Cecil "Ed" Hewitt, MMCS, USN (Ret)

The Engineering Department on the USS *Philippine Sea* was made up of the A, B, E, M and R Divisions. The A Division operated and maintained all the auxiliary machinery throughout the ship, including air conditioning, refrigeration, evaporators, heating, hydraulic elevators, air compressors, steering gear, winches, galley and laundry equipment. The B Division operated and maintained the boilers that generated all the steam for driving the ship, and ship's use in the galley, laundry, heating, etc. The E Division maintained all the electrical equipment throughout the ship. This included all lighting, electric motors, telephones, switchgear, miles of wiring

2 Oct 1946. One of the fighter Planes crashed into the barriers this afternoon...Plane stopped in No. 5 barrier. Please was cleared off Flight Deck and pilot took off in another plane. (Courtesy of Marvin Ferrell.)

and telephone cable. The M Division operated and maintained the main engines for driving the ship through the water, and the turbo generators that generated the electricity for ships use. The R Division ran the carpenter and plumbing shops and was responsible for damage control throughout the ship. My good friend John Hagen, EM1 was in the E Division and took care of the electrical problems on our refrigeration and air-conditioning equipment.

In 1950 as the ship was leaving Quonset Point for San Diego, I was a short timer and planning on getting out in September 1950 after nine years in the Navy. I took my Buick back to Ohio to leave it, then my brother drove me to Pittsburgh, where John Faucet and I caught a plane back to Providence. My friend Raymond Shaw, MM1 had a Nash, that looked like a turned over bathtub, and a Harley Davidson motorcycle. I helped him load them on the *Phil Sea* for the trip to San Diego. When we arrived in San Diego, we set off to explore San Diego in Shaw's Nash, accompanied by J.L. Raines, MM1 and Aycock, HM1 We didn't get very far until Shaw got stopped by one of San Diego's cops for making an improper turn. I then took over the driving and within a short time I got stopped by a motorcycle cop for making a wrong turn. This was too much for J.L. Raines, so he got out and gave the cop a piece of his mind. I still got a ticket though.

We soon determined that the San Diego Cops didn't like sailors. The feeling was mutual.

When the Korean War broke out, I was a short timer and didn't want to go to Korea. I tried to convince the chief engineer, Commander Sonenshein, that he should get a replacement for me. He sent a request to the bureau but no replacements were to be found. I was considered essential as I was the machinist mate in charge of refrigeration and air conditioning. The whole Engineering Department was undermanned. The chief engineer asked for 150 extra men to stand watches and man the department. None were available, so we got 150 Airedales from Miramar Naval Air Station. I wound up with three third class aviation rates, and they turned them into refrigeration and air-conditioning mechanics. I believe it was seven or eight months before we finally got replacements for them and sent them back to Miramar. In August of 1950 as my time was getting short, our President, Harry Truman, extended all military personnel for one year. That did it for me. I decided if I was going to have to stay to fight another war I might as well ship over and get my re-enlistment bonus, so I re-enlisted for six more years. That is how I became a career Navy man.

My air conditioning and refrigeration crew consisted of Wood, MM2; Drewniak, MM3; Quinto, FN; Ishee, FN; Smith, FN; Johnson, FN; Norton, MM3; Anderson, MM3; Ott, FN; Dietz, MM3 and Miller, MM1. C.G. Wright was the A Division yeoman and he talked me into persuading the division officer to let him come work for me in refrigeration and air conditioning. He became the scuttlebutt (water cooler) specialist. You could see him running around the ship cleaning scuttlebutts and making sure the water was cold. We developed a cleaning solution that C.G. poured through the drain each month to kill the bacteria from all the guys spitting in them. Every time I drink at a public water cooler, I wonder if any of them are cleaned the way C.G. used to do them. I ran across C.G. again in Norfolk in 1960. He was a chief machinist's mate. I had a very good crew and I wonder if the Navy men of today are as dedicated as we were back then.

Paul Hitchcock, MM1, ran the Hydraulic Elevator Gang and taught all the younger men how to play poker by holding training sessions in the After Auxiliary every payday. The next day you could find Hitchcock at the post office buying money orders. Nick Vardakis, MM2, and Coats, MM3, was in the Elevator Gang. There was a regular crap game by the ice boxes, above the ice machines every payday. We had one Airedale by the Name of Sweeney, AB3, that was a regular winner. When the ship was ready to return to San Francisco, Sweeney ordered a new Cadillac convertible and the dealer was on the dock to meet him as the ship pulled in. The next day the San Francisco papers read. "A sailor aboard *Philippine Sea* saves pay and buys new Cadillac." It was our money that he saved.

J.L. Raines ran the machine shop. Shaw was the A Division PPO, John Hrabica, MM1 ran the evaporators and kept us supplied with fresh water. Sam Wormsley, ENC, was in charge of the Diesel Gang. Bill Sanger, EN2; Frank Murphy, FN, and Earl Packard, EN3, was in the Diesel Gang. I remember Sanger took care of the boat engines and in the early days they were the boat engineers that ran the boats that took us on liberty. George Dixon, MM2 ran the air compressors. Dixon stayed in the Navy and was a plank owner on the USS *Independence* (CV-62) with me from 1958-60. He was the Elevator Gang Chief on the *Independence*.

Hitchcock, Shaw, Hrabica and some of our Airedale buddies celebrated my 28th birthday at the Yokosuka Naval Base P.O. Club on March 24, 1951.

I recall when one of our planes shot down a Russian plane off Korea. Our men picked up his body and brought him aboard ship and stored him in our meat boxes until we got back in port, at which time he was taken to the Russian Embassy in Tokyo. I had a couple refrigeration men who were afraid to check the ice boxes while he was in there. I told them, " The dead ones' won't hurt you, you have to look out for the live ones."

When we arrived in the San Francisco Naval Shipyard in 1951, I went back to Ohio and married a young woman and brought her back to San Francisco. We lived in naval housing in the shipyard and each night we had a beer party at my house, Hitchcock's house or one of our other shipmates. When the Medical De-

partment required everyone to get a chest x-ray in August of 1951, I wound up in the Naval Hospital at Oaknoll with spots on my lungs. After six to eight weeks of x-rays and tests I was returned to duty with a diagnosis of cause unknown. Years later it was determined to be from breathing asbestos fibers. Anyway I wasn't very happy to be spending my Stateside time in the hospital. They made sure I got back in time to make the return trip to Korea in January 1952. I stayed on the *Phil Sea* until June 1952, when I got orders to push boots at the Naval Training Center. I rode back to San Francisco on the *USS Widham Bay*, a converted troop transport. I stood watches on the turbo-generators, so I got better treatment than some passengers going back. I got in a big Black Jack game, run by one of the ship's company shysters, and came off in San Francisco a few thousand dollars ahead. I was afraid I wasn't going to get off alive with all that money.

I have kept in touch with George Dixon, Clyde Colby, John Hanko, Bill Sanger, Paul Bricker, Tommy Hale, Adrian Hart, John Hagen and a few of the many friends I had on the *Phil Sea*. My wife and I had a wonderful visit with Clyde and Inez Colby in June 1996. They showed us all the wonderful things in Maine, Vermont and New Hampshire. A few of us, including Clyde Colby, Leo Hayden, Mike Huebner, John Faucet, Leonard Allen, Linton Doucet, Adrian Hart and Ralph McGinnis got together in Branson, Missouri in October 1996. It was the first time I had seen Faucet or McGinnis in more than 40 years. We all had a wonderful time. If I left anyone out it wasn't intentional. My memory isn't as good as it used to be. I am 75 years old and have seen my share of good and bad times. I will always cherish my good friends from the USS *Philippine Sea* and remember the good times we had together.

Sailor's Stories
Robert J. Irwin

I was a member of the original crew of the USS *Philippine Sea* and have a plank owner certificate which states that I own a plank on the flight deck. I trained at Newport, Rhode Island and joined the ship in Boston. We had a shakedown cruise in the Caribbean and then were assigned to Admiral Byrd's South Pole expedition, Operation Highjump. We sailed for Cuba and then through the Panama Canal and into the Pacific Ocean headed for Antarctica.

I remember seeing Admiral Byrd taking his daily walk on the flight deck and also crossing the equator when we pollywogs were initiated to the rank of shellback. We crossed the Antarctic Circle on 24 January 1947, the first carrier ever to do so. There were many icebergs around and when we entered the Bay of Whales, the spoutings could be seen for miles. We watched a helicopter crash into the sea and the rescue of the three man crew. We saw Admiral Byrd leave ship on a R4D plane bound for Little America. The ship remained there a short time and then returned to the U.S.

Her Majesty
by Marv Johansen

How proud she is, how gallant rides
Her hull awash, against the tides

Who is this queen, which men have built
At anchor rests, night skies her quilt

Tomorrow sails, at dawns first light
Across the seas, the foe to fiqht

Aboard her dwells, of city-size
A group of men, her country's prize

Each one of these, a specialist
In his own job, he does insist

'Tis with this team, our lady speeds
Fast o'er the waves, to do fair deeds

Aggression stop, far from our shores
To keep the peace, halt unjust wars
From off her decks, like eagles fly
Her cream of crop, men of the sky

To navigate, exact and true
To target spot, O'er ocean blue

Their ordnance drop, to ground below
Blast ammo dump, destroy the foe

If intercept'd, high in the sky
Dogfights occur, and airmen die

As swift they struck, as fast return
To mobile base, whose wake does churn

The LSO, his birds does trap
As high above, orbits the CAP

Yes, majesty, describes this queen
No question this, once she is seen

Sailor Stories
by W.L. Kerns

In 1952 on line in Korean waters, the *Phil Sea* was recovering aircraft when two yeoman third class from the Engineers Office - namely, Bill Kearns and Bob Cossett, had delivered memo's to both the Exec's Office in the superstructure, who decided to watch recovery operations from one of the catwalks on the 04 deck.

The last plane, a crippled Corsair shot up and with only one wheel down, came in for a landing. It missed the catch cables and hopscotched down the flight deck hitting the 5" gun mounts and finally stopping almost under us.

It happened so fast, we didn't have time to move. Needless to say, we went below and changed shorts!

The Marine Detachment

The Marine Detachment aboard the *Phil Sea* consisted of two officers and about 70 enlisted men. They were a close-knit unit with a "It's us against them" attitude. In 1949 and 1950 they were assigned the 20 mm anti-aircraft batteries located fore and aft just below the flight deck. There were about 50 private first class known as "Peons." I think there were six corporals and six sergeants. We had two officers. Captain Conway, who later was promoted to major, and First Lieutenant Straner.

Two of the interesting sergeants aboard at that time were Sergeant Dan Hill from Florida. He enlisted in the Marine Corps in 1943 at the age of (documented) 15! He fought at Iwo Jima, Chosin Reservoir in Korea, and two tours in Vietnam. He won the Bronze Star in Vietnam and retired as sergeant major after 30 years service. He died of prostate cancer a few years ago.

Another sergeant who served in WWII with distinguished service was Sergeant Neil Stiles. Neil was with "Carlson's Raiders" and was on the landing at Makin Island early in 1942. We had another notable sergeant who had been aboard in 1947-48. Sergeant Benedetto had been captured on Wake Island at the start of WWII and had spent the war in a Japanese prison camp. What role models these men were!

Two detachment members I'd served with in 1948 and 1949 were selected to attend Flight School in Pensacola. PFC William McCool was from Jamestown, New York, and flew a Grumman Panther Jet in Korea. He was shot down by ground fire but gained enough altitude to get out into the China Sea to ditch. He was badly injured in the crash landing but was lucky enough to be picked up by Korean fishermen. He returned to the States and did two tours of duty in Vietnam, flying more than 200 missions without a scratch. He retired as a colonel.

The other member who went to Flight School wasn't as lucky. PFC John B. Goery, from Galeton, Pennsylvania, was shot down and killed in Korea. He was flying close air support for the troops. He was flying an F4U Corsair.

We peons (PFCs) were mostly 17 and 18 years of age and fresh out of boot camp. After Parris Island we were selected (Cream of the Crop!) for sea duty. We were sent to Sea School in Portsmouth, Virginia. After six or eight weeks schooling, including gunnery practice at Dam Neck, Virginia, we were assigned to a ship. At that time Marine Detachments were assigned duty on battleships, aircraft carriers, heavy and light cruisers and to flagships.

As we were just out of boot camp and on our first duty assignment we were "Gung Ho" and easy to keep in line. The man who was in charge of us was Gunnery Sergeant Frank Callahan. Frank was only about 30 but he was big, had a broken nose and looked like a Marine "Gunny." Especially to us. He put the fear of God into most of us. I didn't find out until 40 years later that he was a pussy cat.

The *Philippine Sea* had a pistol team. We didn't get to practice much but early in 1950

Courtesy of H. Flint Ranney.

we had defeated Brown University in Providence. En route to the West Coast we defeated the Fleet Marine Force team in Norfolk. The Korean War brought an end to this competition, at least for the length of the war. Members of the team were First Lieutenant Straner, PFCs Richard Thomas and Ralph Lund from Pennsylvania, PFC Jerry Walker of Michigan, PFC Jesse Lane from Vermont, and Seaman Wilbert G. Meisel of V-2 Division. Our coach was Sergeant Nixon who was later killed in Korea. (Back in the 1940s and 1950s, colleges had pistol teams, rifle teams, and even boxing teams. Those were the days!)

In my job as captain's orderly and driver, I spent many hours on the bridge while we were at sea. Captain Waller was my boss and a nicer man I have yet to meet. He treated his orderlies with patience and kindness. I think he was harder on young ensigns than on enlisted personnel. After a while even I could tell who was sharp and who was not. I was enthralled with Air Operations; always interested in aircraft and we were aboard at a great time as the Navy carriers transitioned from propeller aircraft to jets. My favorite planes were the Grumman F8F Bearcats and the Vought F4U Corsairs. My General Quarters station was in the forward 20mm mount. It was next to the Starboard Catapult. Very interesting to watch the jets being shot off just a few yards away. A great time to be "Young and Dumb" - my two years aboard the *Phil Sea* were two of the best years of my young life.

I'm not sure of the dates but en route to the West Coast we called at Norfolk. This was about the time the USS *Missouri* went aground in Chesapeake Bay. I was on the bridge as Captain R.R. Waller's orderly. Everyone in authority on the bridge was nervous. Commander David was the navigator and every few minutes Captain Waller would ask him, "Are you sure, Dave?" Then they would both go to the chart room to check the charts again. I got the feeling that Captain Waller didn't trust the navigator that much!

Going through the Panama Canal en route to San Diego was interesting but the weather was very hot. I remember it would rain for 10 minutes then the sun would come out and steam you until it rained again. We had liberty in Panama but I don't remember much about it. Not a place you'd want to visit again.

When we arrived in San Diego (The Norfolk of the West) we were all eager to go ashore. Most everyone headed for Tijuana! A few of us discovered National City, about halfway between San Diego and Tijuana. A short bus ride. We discovered a nightspot that played jazz and country. I remember there was a very good band with about five banjos.

On 15 June 1950, about 10 of us were transferred off the ship as our two-year tour was completed. We were sent to China Lake, California, for duty at the Naval Ordnance Test Station. On 25 June the Korean War started and we would have been the first to go with the Division. China Lake was out in the Mojave Desert and was a Guided Missile Testing Station. The base was bigger than Rhode Island and you had to have a top security clearance to work there - we were security. I spent the rest of my time in the Corps there and although I hated it, it was a lot safer than Korea! I returned home in 1952 to get married and joined the NYC Fire Department in 1955, to serve 36 years and then retired to beautiful Bucks County (Pennsylvania) in 1990 with the hope of living "Happily Ever After."

OPERATION HIGHJUMP
by Edward E. Nugent

Regardless of how proud we may be of our service aboard USS *Philippine Sea* CV-47 our memory of events usually lacks the type of information that would make it an accurate historical record. With this in mind I believe such a historical record should be included of our ships involvement in the famous Operation Highjump. Since I am a former crew member who recently did considerable research to write a story for the *Foundation* magazine of the National Museum of Naval Aviation, perhaps I am the one to prepare this brief but historically accurate account or this page in history, that *Phil Sea's* role will not be forgotten.

Courtesy of Flint Ranney.

Late in 1946 the *Phil Sea* was loaded with six Douglas R4D-5s, a Sikorsky HO3S-1 and two Consolidated OY-1s. *The Phil Sea* lost her HO3S helicopter on a takeoff 22 January 1947 before rendezvousing With Task Force 68. Fortunately the crew was rescued.

The R4Ds of course are the planes most remembered historically. Their wing span was greater than that of the B-25s used in the Doolittle Raid from *Hornet* (CV-8); therefore they could only use the 400 feet of the flight deck forward of the island.

Ironically, most of these. R4D pilots and copilots had never flown an aircraft of any kind from a carrier, and time did not permit any practice flights. The fact that the R4D flights would be "one way" is not, usually pointed out. Robert Cressman in his article, on the *Phil Sea* in *The Hook* (Fall 1988) was an exception when he frankly stated that the six R4Ds were "abandoned on the ice" after Byrd finished with them. It must be remembered that this was right after, World War II, and a huge number of these old "workhorses" existed. Many would be around for some time to come, but, for me it is nice to know these six Skytrains have "outfoxed" the ravishes of time under their blanket of snow and ice. (Although many believe by now the ice movement has added them all to the sea.)

The Coast Guard icebreaker *Northwind* led the way through Ross Sea for *Mount Olympus* and the cargo ships *Yancey* (AKA-93) and *Merrick* (AKA-97) for establishment or the base called Little America. For accuracy Little America was in fact Little America IV. The location of "Little America" varied for each expedition.

Once the base was established an airstrip was laid down to accommodate the R4Ds that would fly 800 miles from the deck of *Philippine Sea*. For the initial fly-in, the aircraft would use dual landing gear of two skis on each side separated by a space wide enough for the wheel. The wheel then protruded three inches below the level of the skis. The CO of *Phil Sea*, Captain Delbert S. Cornwell, would have preferred six inches of the wheel below the ski for a safer carrier take-off but this would have made wheel-ski landing on the ice and snow impossible. The skis were not as long as RADM Byrd would have preferred for the ski landing but if they were any longer a carrier takeoff would be impossible.

The spectacular sight of the first R4D Skytrains lifting off the carrier deck occurred 29 Jan 1947. RADM Byrd was in the first plane piloted by CDR William M. "Trigger" Hawkes. Four JATO bottles, scarcely larger than a standard fire extinguisher, were mounted on the sides of the planes. The planes started rolling very slowly, but when the JATO bottles were fired, they quickly lifted into the air.

Interestingly, Byrd wrote (in 1947) of this takeoff, stating that an unassisted takeoff would be possible with a redesigned flight deck." He did not elaborate. Did he in his mind's eye see the angle deck? These were also years when most politicians believed only long-range bombers were the answer for future wars and RADM Byrd correctly pointed out that Operation Highjump demonstrated that carriers were not obsolete, and gave the Navy a great public relations boost.

The decision was made that all six R4Ds would not be put at risk on the same day. After the first two landed safely at Little America, the other four were flown in the next day.

The planes had been made as light as possible including the removal of oxygen equipment for high-altitude flying. After their arrival in Little America, the Skytrains wheels were removed and the space left open by their removal was covered. Many still had doubts about the planned flights.

When it was time for the first flight the plane would not budge even with the engines at full throttle. The plane was then rocked, but still it would not break loose. Finally, planks were worked under the skis to start the plane moving. JATO bottles were mounted at the last minute, as it was believed the extreme cold would cause their premature firing. Each problem was simply faced as it arose until the procedure was smooth.

The Skytrains flew 29 operational flights for a total of 27,500 miles in just two weeks. Numerous cameras on each plane made detailed mapping possible. These photos were also compared with earlier photos to reveal changes in the Ross Ice Barrier and the rate and direction of the movement of the ice formations. Nine of the flights were not productive, as they were plagued by weather or mechanical problems. Other problems encountered included failure of aircraft heating system and anoxia due lack of oxygen, the result of the earlier removal of oxygen equipment. A runway of "marston matting" was laid out and one R4D operated with wheels and no skis making flights limited to the Little America area.

RADM Byrd helped Naval Aviation enhance its image through difficult political years while pursuing his passion as an explorer. The USS *Philippine Sea* CV-47 was selected for her key role because she was at that time the newest and the best. The impact on our Navy is still alive today despite the fact, Operation Highjump is forgotten by most.

POSSIBLE RETRIBUTION: AN INTERNATIONAL EVENT
by Frank L. Allender

On 24 May 1950, the USS *Philippine Sea* began exercising its orders to be transferred from the East Coast to the West Coast. The ship got underway from Norfolk at 10:07 a.m. to proceed through the Panama Canal to its West Coast destination - San Diego.

As a radarman life aboard the ship was interesting, challenging and rewarding. For sure I was good for 20 years. It was a peacetime Navy; the food was great and the accommodations were comfortable, and, as promised by my recruiter, I was "seeing the world." Soon, I dreamed, I would be visiting the Hawaiian Islands and ports-of-call in the Orient. Things were going even better than I expected.

Who on the ship at the time could or would have even dared to think that one month and a day after leaving Norfolk for San Diego, we would, while leaving the Long Beach Harbor, 25 June 1950, be alerted to the fact that the North Koreans had invaded South Korea. For sure, this act quickly and radically changed the life style and mission of the U.S. Navy for years to follow. The USA essentially had gone to war again less than four years and 10 months from the signing of the "article of surrender," aboard the USS *Missouri*, officially ending WWII on 2 September 1945.

I remember that day, 25 June 1950, because I was standing duty on the bridge manning the radar repeater as the ship was leaving the Long Beach Harbor. A messenger, I believe it was a Marine, handed the captain notice of the invasion. "Watertight integrity" was set immediately. No panic occurred, but instantly I knew big changes were in store for both the ship and her crew. Life aboard the *Philippine Sea* changed dramatically. It now began to operate with a sense of urgency.

After loading ammunition and taking on an Air Group in San Diego, the *Phil Sea* headed for "Buckner Bay," via a stopover in Hawaii, to join Task Force 77, that was 24 July 1950. The admiral said, "The Valley Forge needs you and you are ready to go after seeing today's operations. So, I'm sending you to a point off Okinawa as fast as the ship is capable. Good luck to all of you." The *Phil Sea* would not see the shores of the "mainland" again until 9 June 1951 when it returned from operating with TF-77 off of Korea. The *Phil Sea* powered its way under the Golden Gate Bridge at 1202, approximately 320 days after it left San Diego to join TF-77 in the Western Pacific. That was a long time to be away from the USA. The dramatics at times were equal to World War II: Death, bravery, sacrifices, heroics, ingenuity, stupidity, cruelness, kindness, hate and love. The most constant emotion was fear, although subtle, more so sometimes than others, it was available for handling the ever constant critical operations of the ship. The USS *Philippine Sea* had its fair share of scared.

The most dramatic day and/or incident for me was on 4 September 1950. While standing watch in CIC our radar picked up a "bogey" on screen 58 miles away from our TF-77. We tracked it up to 28 miles from the TF whereupon our CAP intercepted it. Our CAP reported it had a red star on it and asked permission to shoot. Permission was granted and it was shot down. The pilot reported it had a painted nose, was a twin engine with single tail, and the wings were almost inverted gull. Our destroyer, *Tomcat*, picked up the pilot and found him to be Russian. He probably died of bullet wounds which had been inflicted. This was an international affair with questionable consequences.

That same evening without fanfare, the body of the Russian pilot was brought aboard

July 7, 1958. Capt. Tuttle paints "E" on mount 57. Gunnery Dept. observes. LTJG Ranney is on left.

Aboard USS Philippine Sea.

about 8:00 p.m. No word was passed to "man the transfer station." They transferred him to sick bay. For identification purposes, pictures were taken of his face and hands only. On the back of one hand was a tattoo of a bird sitting on a limb. Yes, the pilot's body was returned to the Russians via destroyer transfer in the Sea of Vladivostok. Ironically, the next night, 5 September 1950, a single "bogey" came in over the TF-77. Our ship was having a movie, the first in about two weeks. General quarters sounded bringing that activity to an end. An off-center blast was fired. That incident scared us. I thought the Russians were taking retribution for our downing of their pilot. We never did find out who or what passed over our TF-77; it's difficult to believe even when I read my diary as I write, but I do remember that day very distinctly.

Phil Sea - A Real Steamer
by Al Atwell

There are few that will deny that *Phil Sea* (CV-47) was a "real steamer" - a "can do" ship that met every commitment and got every job done in a very professional manner. But there were also some other interesting things that I recall during my short tour aboard *Phil Sea* (October 48-July 51).

For starters, when I reported aboard at Quonset Point, she was loading and making preps to get underway for pre-deployment air groups quals and work-up. There were so many new people checking aboard that about 100 of us were required to sleep in "hammocks" swung from the overhead of the mess deck. I thought wow, this is going to be an interesting tour. Finally, after a few days when some personnel were flown-off the ship, all of the new arrivals were assigned regular bunks in their assigned division spaces.

I was thankful to get a bunk in the OI division space which was just aft of the island and just under the flight deck. Being the new kid on the block, I was assigned the top bunk which was located immediately under a large cross-deck pendant rewind reel, which was a very noisy piece of equipment during flight ops. But later when I observed prop blades occasionally cutting through the flight deck into our living space during hard landings or crashes, I felt very fortunate to bunk under this very sturdy and protective piece of equipment.

After about 90 days of seemingly non-stop ops and airgroup work-ups, we departed Quonset for a six-month Mediterranean deployment. We got our first liberty, Gibraltar, and after getting underway cross-decked some Royal Navy Marine Spit Fires aboard *Phil Sea*. We noted one of these Seafires make a hard landing which broke-off a piece of the wooden propeller blade. We were amazed to see them taxi the aircraft onto our #2 elevator, shut down the engine, saw-off the ends of the other two prop-blades to get a rough balance in length/weight, then quickly crank it up and fly-off.

With daily day/night flight ops, general drills, and other continuing ships work, we had routinely settled-in to an 18 hour workday and it looked like it was going to be a long cruise. But very abruptly, we were ordered to drop anchor off the French coast near Nice/Cannes and reduce expenditures to a minimum. Congress had not passed the new year appropriations bill and we ended up with liberty call on the Riviera Coast for almost a month, where more than one Phil Sea trooper fell in love with France.

Finally the funds were authorized and we completed a very busy Med deployment and returned to Quonset Point, and after a bit of leave and liberty, began routine training ops. When I first checked aboard *Phil Sea* in late 1948, all of our aircraft were prop types. But we soon got involved in testing and OpEvals of the oncoming jet aircraft: F9F, F2H, etc. Most aircraft worked out OK but I particularly remember the fleet CV tests for the F2H Banshee. It was a hot aircraft with a very high landing speed. After experiencing numerous tail hook failures, broken cross-deck pendants and some deck crashes that penetrated the barriers and severely damaged numerous aircraft spotted forward of the barriers and severely damaged numerous aircraft spotted forward of the barriers, it was quickly determined that the F2H was just too hot for the Essex Class straight deck CV.

A few months later, we found out that our home port was being changed to Alameda, California. After completing some busy ops with LantFlt, we departed for PacFlt via the Panama Canal.

Since we were the last Essex Class CV built, we anticipated no problems in transiting the canal as many other Essex Class CVS had routinely transited the canal without incident. But to everyone's surprise *Phil Sea* got stuck tight in one of the canal locks. Apparently, as the Navy had continued to add more people, aircraft and equipment aboard our carriers, our draft had increased enough to cause *Phil Sea's* overhanging sponsons to hang up firmly in the lock. It took a large team of cutters and welders to cut-away enough sponsons, catwalks, etc. to free the ship and enable us to proceed to PacFlt.

About the same time frame, we got word that North Korea had invaded South Korea and we were soon heading west at 27 kts embarking a new airgroup along the way. As a result of much dedicated planning, training and pure hard work, the *Phil Sea* team performed superbly off-Korea. But it soon became obvious that maybe we were too good.

We were supposed to be home in our new homeport by Xmas, but it didn't happen. After completing our six-month deployment we were invited to extend it for another six months to fill-in for a scheduled replacement CV that couldn't make it.

The winter weather up along the Korean coast was mostly severe with strong winds and high sea states as a result of severe cold fronts that swept through the area approximately every four days. When it got too rough to conduct flight ops, we would head south for some heavy weather replenishment. On one occasion, an unidentified twin-engine bomber suddenly emerged out of a low overcast very close to our formation. Our combat air patrol F9F was quickly launched and shot it down. It appeared to be a North Korean aircraft provided by the Russians along with a Russian pilot. It was somewhat of a surprise to note that the recovered body of the soviet flyer had some stainless steel teeth.

As the combat cruise was extended past six months, *Phil Sea* was ordered to swap-out some air group aircraft with another CV that was returning to CONUS. The weather was bad for three to four days with very strong winds and high sea states. After several days of waiting and considerable frustration, *Phil Sea* and the other CV got their aircraft in the air for swapout. We were occasionally taking large swells over the bow and the fantail was rising and falling approximately 2030 feet making for a real hairy landing situation. Making a long story short, we pranged about 15-20 aircraft as they dove for the deck while trapping aboard *Phil Sea*.

As we worked into the second six month deployment, it made us look forward to our occasional break in the action when we made a high speed run to either Sasebo or Yokosuka for expedited upkeep. We would conduct approximately 30 days of combat flight ops and then head south at high speed (30 kts plus) without escort to the shipyard where we got about five days of urgent work accomplished.

For our ship's company snipes, this five day R&R for most of the crew, was harder work than while on the line. And it was also a real challenge for the CIC/NAV team getting *Phil Sea* through Tsushima Straits at night doing 30+ kts without running over some small craft/vessels.

Finally, more than 12 months after we had left our previous home port, *Phil Sea* headed east, to our new homeport in Alameda. Our snipes were tired but ready for one more challenge as the ship went after the world record for crossing the Pacific. *Phil Sea* left NavSta Yokohama, Japan early on 1 June 1951 and arrived at NAS Alameda, California, on 9 June, completing the 5,000 NM transit in seven days 13 hours, at an average speed of 27.62 kts.

Yes, the old *Phil Sea* was a real streamer. She had some of the best people I've ever ran across in my Navy career. She was a real "can do" ship that always got the job done, in spite of some of the most demanding challenges.

Mediterranean Cruise
By: Edgar A. Siewert

On January 5, 1948 the Philippine Sea steamed out of the Quonset harbor and headed southward, leaving the frozen wastelands of New England on the horizon for the tropics of Guantanamo Bay, Cuba. Most departments, because of green and inexperienced crews, found they had many obstacles to overcome before they could develop into a smooth running team. Despite such hardships, the ship's progress was rapid during its three weeks in the Caribbean. We became molded into a potential fighting unit.

From Guantanamo we sailed to Norfolk where we were greeted by snow and marines, in that order. The Eighth Marines and the Second Marine Division joined our family aboard ship. We gave up our sleeping quarters for the marines and moved into our work station.

The ship sail back to Quonset Point for some rest and rehabilitation before heading to the Mediterranean by way of Guantanamo Bay. We rendezvoused with other ships of our task force and proceeded with fleet exercises while enroute to the Caribbean. Then for five days and nights we besieged the enemy forces located on Vieques Island, east of Puerto Rico, blasting them with everything we had, from machine-gun bullets to water bombs. The Marines moved ashore mopping up the remnants of the enemy garrison. We detached from the Second Task Fleet and headed Eastward to the Mediterranean.

On 1 March we arrived at Gibraltar and relieved the *USS Midway*. From the bay on the west side of Gibraltar it looks like a loaf of bread with a wrinkled top, but from the north or south it looks like Prudential Life Insurance Company's trademark. The rock itself has a gun for every day of the year surrounding it and tunnels to get to them, so the British say. On the west side of the rock is the City of Gibraltar. Here we had our first go at using foreign money. We also met the rest of the Sixth feet. We already had an Admiral on our ship so the fleet Admiral chose a cruiser for his flag ship and brought his own sail boat.

The next place we stopped was Bone, now Annaba, Algeria in North Africa. Before the ship would land in a country we would be given a briefing on the countries customs and courtesies that should be given the people. One of the things we were told was that in North Africa, Hobos didn't carry their things in a bag over their shoulders but in the crotch of their pants. If we happened to see one of them, don't laugh that would be an insult.

Camp and I went on pass where we saw some of the sights, cathedrals, markets, and people that looked like Masons with their little, red fez caps. Then we went for a walk out in the country. Walking down a dusty country road we came upon one of the Hobos with everything in his crotch, one of the funniest sights I'd ever seen. When we were about a hundred yards apart the Hobo looked at the two of us sailors and started to laugh. He pointed at us and jabbered something in his own language and laughed and laughed. So we laughed back at him. Guess he had never seen a sailor and we had never seen a Hobo with such a big crotch. After we all quit laughing we went on our different ways.

The Arabic women wore costumes that covered their entire body, except for one small peephole located at either the right or left side of their face, depending on which was their good eye. For us, it was an education.

After being out to sea a few days we dropped anchor off of Sfax, Tunisia, way off Sfax, about nine to twelve miles off. When I first looked at Sfax from my shop it looked like a beach in the distance but when we took the liberty boat into it, there was a small city. This was our first introduction to the Kasbah, the walled off city. Of course it was off limits to us because white men never came out alive or so they said.

They used mud fences with cactus on top to keep a people from crawling over but the camels ate the cactus like it was grass, needles and all. The camels were as popular as a pickup in Oklahoma and used the same way, with almost as much of a load carrying capacity.

I did take a bus tour, the chaplin had arraigned, to El Jem north of Sfax about forty miles where there is an old coliseum. It is somewhat smaller than Rome's but well preserved. One of the largest in the Roman world, seating 35,000. El Jem was Thysdus to the Romans. I brought some coins that were melted

Audience with Pope Pius. Not all the sailors are from the USS Philippine Sea, but some are. (Courtesy of J.P. Greene.)

together and blackened from fire, that were found at the coliseum, during the time of the Roman Occupation, the man told me. But when I got some of the black cleaned off them, back at the ship, they were from eighteen hundreds.

Our next port of call was Argostoli on the island of Cephalonia, the west side of Greece. The rugged mountains of the island slope acutely into the natural harbor where we anchored with all the fleet, three cruisers and eight destroyers. The town of Argostoli was small, about 1000 people, and sat on a peninsula. Which we were restricted to because of the war between the Greek Nationalist and Communist. It took an afternoon to see the town but it turned out to be our Guantanamo of the Mediterranean.

We were in and out of there frequently. Because this was the year that the State of Israel was formed we world run to Argostoli every time our government thought we might have to evacuate Americans from Israel or that area. This crewed up a lot of good liberty in place lake France and Italy.

Argostoli was the only place we were that had a war going on. One Sunday morning, I woke up to a "pop, pop, pop" over in the mountains as I walked up to the bridge where there is a large mounted set of binoculars. They were about 35 power and I swung them to the east to see a war going on in the mountains. At night I would see and hear large gun fire in the mountains. At gobs below decks weren't bothered with this kind of stuff, they couldn't hear it.

Every time we went into Argostoli the ship had all the gun tubs loaded with ammo and those in the open were covered with gray canvas so you couldn't tell they were full. We had four night fighter airplanes on board and they were ready for launching in 15 minutes. If a round would have hit the fleet we could have stopped their war in the short time on that island.

One time in Argostoli the ship leased a beach from an individual and ran our liberty boats directly there, so we didn't have to be in dress uniform for the beach party. The ship even furnished two cans of beer for each man. the ship paid for the beach with old apple crates or other wood we took over to give the man. Seemed wood was hard for them to come by.

After we had been there for an hour a few locals came around selling brandy in bottles with waxed corks in them. Some of the men hadn't brought any money with them so the locals traded for pieces of uniforms. Camp and I each had a brandy then we noticed these Greeks would kind of wait on the bottles, snatch them up as soon as you were finished and head off up the hill with the empties. After Camp and I had enough swimming we decided to climb up the hill to see what we could see. At the top of the high hill, on the back side, we saw the bottling company. A couple of men had a large crock jug about four feet tall, full of brandy. As the other Greeks returned with the empty bottles they were refilled and another wax cork put in them with no cleaning. Then down the hill to sell it to another unsuspecting gob. As far as I know, nobody caught anything except intoxication.

We had open house for the Greeks while we were there and brought them aboard the ship for a look to see. They still never realized we were armed and ready.

The ship closed off the drains on the port side of the ship while in port and let the crew swim on that side. There is a ladder that runs from the hanger deck to just above the water. It has a landing at the bottom of the ladder to get into and out of the boat, this is where most of us dove and swam from. But there were some that dove from the hanger deck, 30 feet above the water and some that dove from the flight deck, 70 feet above the water.

Malta was the next stop on our tour and it had something we sorely missed in the other countries we had been. Malta offered us people who spoke the English language. This is the country that offered the world the Maltese Cross, the Maltese Cat, and the malted milkshake, I think.

We visited many beautiful churches housing original painting by the great masters, like Michelangelo. The effects of the terrible bombing raids by the Luftwaffe during the war were noticeable wherever we turned. Reconstruction was underway as it was in all of the Mediterranean.

Malta is all rock including the fences which are rock walls. When I first took a taxi drive he scared me to death drivieng so fast down the road with the rock walls so close, just like running a maze, the roads weren't straight. They told us all the dirt on Malta had been shipped in.

I visited St. Paul's Catacombs in Rabat where the Christians lived during the time of persecution. They are under ground and tunneled out of sandstone rock. The entrance had a big rock door, a couple of feet thick, that would swing shut over the tunnel and could be locked. Along the walls of the tunnels people would carve out a place large enough to sleep in, a couple of feet above the floor. When they would marry they carved their place deep enough for two people. As they had a family it was carved wider for them. When a person would die they were put in one of these holes, closed up, and plastered shut. There was central cooking room with a dome in the middle and a hole in the dome to let the smoke out, and a fire pit under it. These tunnels fanned out in different directions and one even went to the sea a mile away.

Back to sea for us, passing between Sicily and Italy and right by the Island of Stromboli. There was an erupting volcano on it, the first I had ever seen. We sailed on east and north passed Corsica into the Gulf of Hyeres, on the southern coast of France where the ship anchored. Some ships weren't as lucky as the *Philippine Sea.* Two cruisers had to go to Cannes, and a third, the fleet's admiral, was forced to make liberty in the nasty old city of Nice.

The second Invasion of southern France was on when liberty call was sounded. We were restricted to Hyers and Toulon but some of the men went to Marseille anyway. When they returned, the ship had moved to Toulon which is ten miles away. Not only were they late, but they had missed the ship in the foreign country. Luckily they ran into some of the crew in Toulon and made it back with only minor penalties.

Toulon is where the French scuttled its fleet when they were captured by the Germans in World War II. Every were you looked, you could see tops of ships that were sunk, I think I counted over forty and some had already been removed or were completely covered with water.

This was the best liberty yet. The ship offered tours to Marseille, Monte Carlo, Nice, and Paris in addition to perfume factories and other points of interest. *The Philippine Sea* had a ship's dance and invited French ladies on board to enjoy it and the ship's band, who played. This was to have lasted two weeks but things got worse in Israel so in three days we left.

While we were there one of the meteorologists and I went to a nice restaurant to eat. They had told us not to drink the water because it was still contaminated from the war. The waitress didn't speak English and we didn't speak French, so we just picked something on the menu. Then she wanted to know what we wanted to drink. The wine made me sick so I said, "Champagne." She then kept asking something but we didn't know what.

She said, "Wait," and left. Shortly she came back with six bottles of champagne in a basket all dusty from the wine cellar. She would dust one off, put it on the table and point to that kind on the menu, then to the next. This didn't mean anything to us because we weren't familiar with any of the champagnes, but she set one down that was 99 years old and that was the one we took. That was made before the Civil War, probably before there were any Siewerts of my family in the USA. That champagne went down as smooth as water but when we left the restaurant and got two blocks away it got us.

We left Toulon and headed east between Corsica and Sardinia but the affairs in Israel must have changed because we stopped in Naples, Italy. Where they tied tug boats to us to take us into the harbor. The Italian pilot that came aboard got our attention when he started hollering over the public address system, "Pussy, Pussy, Pussy." We looked to the starboard and to the port but we didn't see any girls. After the third time he called, "Pussy, Pussy, Pussy," we found out he was telling the tug boat to push.

I took a trip to a cameo factory at the foot of mount Vesuvius, then to Pompeii, and Salerno. Pompeii was the most interesting.

There was a half dozen of us sailors that went through together and a guide, for a small fee, showed us some things that the normal public doesn't get to see, dirty pictures, ect.

In Salerno we met a young boy that got chummy with us. He said, "When the people of Salerno heard the fleet was in Naples they just doubled the prices. So if you want to buy anything just split the price in half and try to talk them down from there." He really was a help.

Two hundred and thirty five of the Catholics sailors made a one day crusade to Rome. The trip was long and tedious but proved to be well worth while. In Rome busses took the group to the Vatican City for a rapid tour through St. Peter's. After viewing this largest Cathedral on the continent, they moved to the Vatican Palace where they were granted an audience with Pope Pius XII. Who spoke briefly with each man and gave them this coin.

Again what was going to be a two weeks stay turned into three days. Our disappointment of leaving Naples after such a short visit was overshadowed by our joyous anticipation of returning to Argostoli for old home week.

From the halls of Argostoli to the shores of Tripoli or how every the song goes, was our next stop on the Mediterranean. Tripoli had much to offer us, many things we hadn't seen in almost a month, such as sand, camel, Arabs, and Kasbah, which was again off limits. It was 115 degrees in the shade, you could spit and it would evaporate before it hit the ground. So they warned us to drink carefully, which we did by sipping it.

The ship couldn't get into the harbor because they had sunk a ship full of concrete in the opening to keep the Germans from using the harbor. We anchored about a mile off shore and shortly after we dropped anchor a fly showed up. Do you suppose he flew all the way from shore.

The ship cranked up all the aircraft and launched them by the catapult, sending them into an Air Force Base in Libya, a short distance from Tripoli. This was the first time I knew they could launch aircraft at anchor. While in Tripoli a lot of the shipboard pilots

Philippine Sea CV47, crew at the Acropolis. Athens, Greece 1949. Courtesy of G. Barr.

that don't normally fly, logged many hours over the sands of Africa keeping qualified, including the ship's Captain.

One of the Air Force pilots in a B24 buzzed the ship making a dive bomb run beside the ship. Then pulling out when he was even with the flight deck, he pulled it up into the air doing a roll our on top. I never knew a four engine airplane could do this.

I visited the ancient Roman ruins of Sabratha, about 30 miles form Tripoli. It was an old Roman city with an amphitheater and other interesting things.

We made a couple trips into Crete which were interesting. But the most interesting thing about it was while I was waiting on the dock for the liberty boat. I looked into the water under the dock, there was a torpedo stuck in the pilings. I waited off the dock after that until the boat arrived. It may have been disarmed but it sure didn't look like it.

All the extra marines we took on board were used to guard the ship in port and to be used as body guard ashore. Every port we went into there would be "bum boats" as we called them, come out to the ships to sell things. Some were so aggressive they would come aboard the ships. The marines stopped them. At night light were strung around the ship so there were no dark place where anyone could hide or come aboard.

On June 14th, the *USS Kearsage* came into Suda Bay, just off Crete, she was our replacement in the 6th Fleet. the following day we had exercises with the Kearsage for joint operations. We were on our way home at last, whereas she was just starting the ordeal.

Part of the cruise had been fun-others had been trying. I was thankful for having seen many interesting places in the Mediterranean, but more thankful we were going home.

I had been taking some course through the United States Armed Forces Education (USAFE) to complete my high school. In June, I took the (GED) General Education Development Test to finally complete it.

On June 26, we arrived at Quonset Point, RI. then spent three weeks in Boston Navy Yards. That summer and fall we were in Operational Development Forces conduction experimental things like testing jets and CCA.

We tested one of the first fleets of jet aircraft, McDonald F2H-2D Banshees. They started their take off run the same place as the other propeller fighter airplanes, which was too short. When they ran off the end of the flight deck the oleo strut the wheels are attached to, dropped from under the airplane, indicating the ship wasn't airborne yet. Then the airplane would drop below the flight deck a little before it was up to flying speed and would climb off. The third airplane to take off when it dropped below the ship, I guess the pilot thought the carrier would run over him, so he banked to the right and stalled. The jet plopped in the water to the right and ahead of the carrier. The pilot got out and straddled the back of the fuselage while he inflated his life raft, then got in it and paddled away, the jet eventually sunk. We had never seen an airplane float as long as that jet. The Bearcat fighters we carried would usually be under water when the pilot got out; they would just hit and sink. Another piece of equipment we tested was Carrier Control Approach (CCA) system. It is the same thing airports use today to bring airplane in by radar and talking them down. The radar ran across the rear of the flight deck, just below it. They spent many clear days talking the pilots in until it was perfect.

We also brought some Army, or Air Force as it was changed to, pilots on for training. They had some navy flying before they came aboard but you could tell the differences they just weren't as sharp as the navy men. Plus, they would get confused at our bugle calls because a lot of them mean different things in the Army and Air Force.

The navy made the movies of the Operation Highjump in the Artarctic called, "The Secret Land." The ship went to New York Harbor on the Hudson where all the big passenger ships docked for the premiere showing. The film was sin color and narrated by Robert Montgomery, Robert Taylor, and Van Heflin. Admiral Richard E. Byrd, Real admiral Richard H. Cruzen co-commander of expedition and the Captains of all the ships in the three fleets were there with a lot of other dignitaries from the navy and civilians. It was quite exciting to be part of it.

One duty weekend I had in Quonset Point the rumor was spread the President was going to dock beside us because they said all the civilians that were aboard ship were Secret Service men. I don't know it they were Secret Service men or not but sure enough the *USS Williamberg* did dock beside us. President Harry S. Truman was standing out in form off the bridge as big as life. I was standing on the flight deck where I got a good look at him and of course we had to salute the Commander-in-Chief. The men that came back from pass asked, "What is going on? Every hundred yards for the main gate to the ship someone stops you to see your ID card and Pass". We told them, the president's yacht's across the dock from us.

The *USS Philippine Sea* was the Atlantic Fleet carrier winner of the Battle Efficiency Pennant the Navy "E" for the first post-war year of competition for the Navy's highest peacetime unit award. Climaxing a relatively short but extremely colorful career.

HAM & EGGS
By: LT "Jocko" Fullerton

It was sometime in December 1950. We had been at sea about a month and a half with continuous operations. The only break was every four or five days we would pull off the line to rearm, refuel and replenish. During replenishment, a couple enterprising members of our catapult crew made off with a ham & several dozen fresh eggs.

All of the catapult crews quarters were in the catapult pump rooms up forward on the 4th deck. The catapult machinery was on the 3rd deck & all of this was located up forward in officers country. Many of the officers were berthed on the 2nd deck, above the catapults & forward of the officers wardroom.

Our division chief was able to cumshaw several loaves of fresh bread and a couple pounds of butter, so the evening of replenishment, on our way back to the line, we set up a kitchen in the port catapult machinery room. All hands of the catapult crew were treated to as many fresh eggs, any style, and ham as they could hold.

Needless to say all the aroma of ham & eggs cooking wafted up into officer country and created a stampede to the wardroom only to find there were no ham & eggs to be had. I do not believe anyone ever did find out where that cooking smell came from.

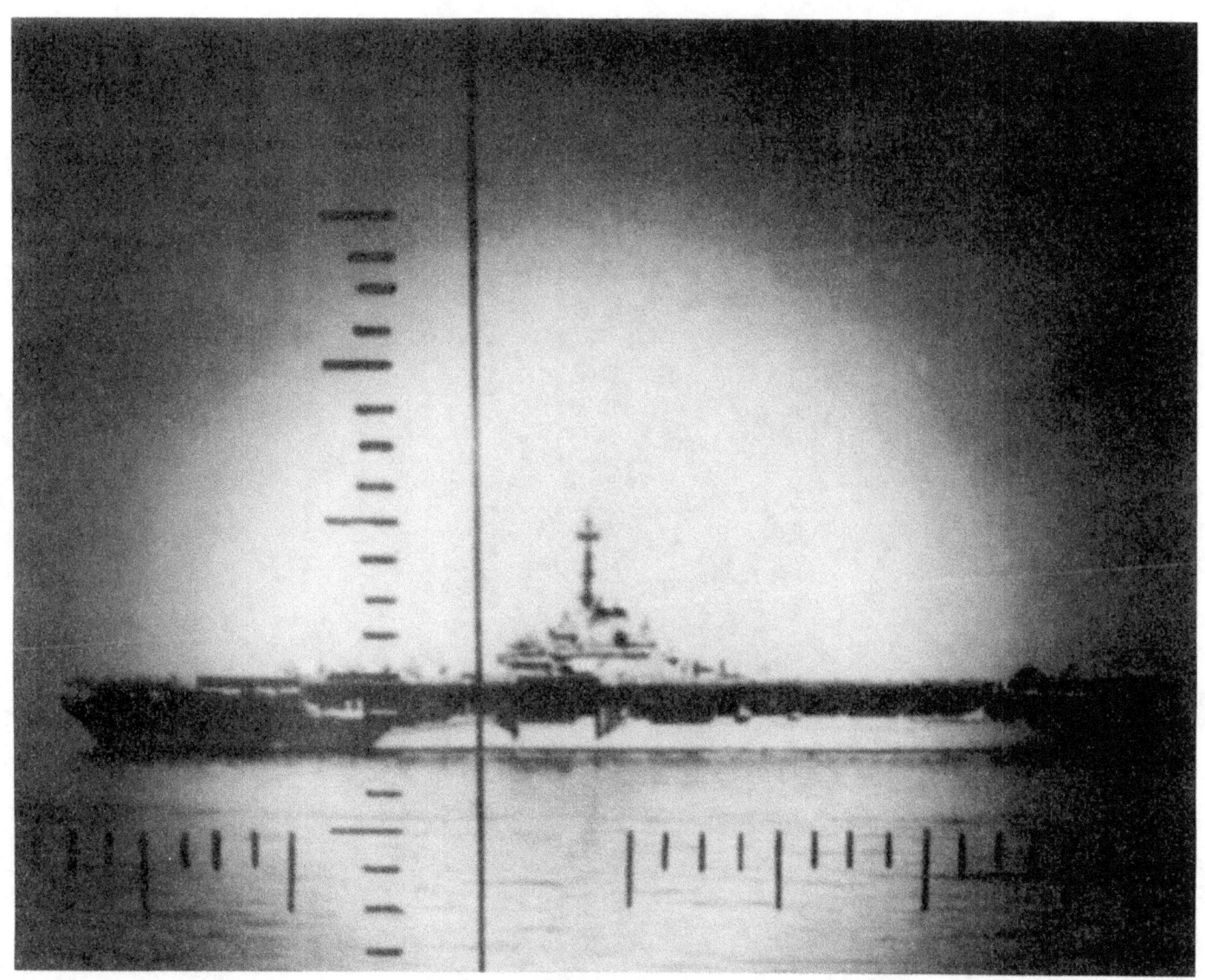

Periscope shot of the Philippine Sea

USS PHILIPPINE SEA VETERANS

JACK M. ABNEY, DK-2, born May 9, 1929, Eastman, GA. Enlisted USN January 1948. Enjoyed boot camp at San Diego NAS, afterward attended Supply School USNTC, San Diego. Chose disbursing as his career objective. Upon graduation in September 1948, assigned a billett aboard USS *Philippine Sea*, stationed at Quonset Point, RI. He served his total Navy time aboard the USS *Philippine Sea*. Was discharged Dec. 21, 1951 in San Diego, CA.

Married Dorethea Sommers of Santa Cruz, CA and raised six children: Gordon, Cheryle, Robin, Stuart, Tina, and Chris and has six grandchildren.

Worked 32 years with Civil Service at Robins AFB, Warner Robins, GA and retired in 1985 to the family farm in Gary, GA outside of Cochran.

FRANK L. ALLENDER, RD2, born Sept. 26, 1930, Orbisonia, PA. Enlisted service: July 1948, boot camp Co. 282, Great Lakes NTC; Radar and CIC School, Norfolk, VA, November 1948-April 1949; boarded USS *Philippine Sea* (CV-47) May 1949, Quonset Point, RI; left ship in Japan June 1952 for San Francisco via troop transport; discharged July 10 at Treasure Island, CA.

Graduated from Penn State University 1956 with BS degree in health education; following, completed 15 month certificate course in physical therapy at Los Angeles Children's Hospital, November 1957. Practiced clinical and rehabilitation physical therapy at various children and Veteran Administration hospitals in Virginia and California until September 1970; and, from 1970-1987, served as director, Annual Conference and Continuing Education Programs for the American Physical Therapy Associations' Headquarter Office, Washington, DC; retired from same November 1987; never married; world traveler.

JACK WADE ANGEL, SN1/c, born Feb. 1, 1929, Wallston, OH, Jackson County. Inducted June 25 1946, Columbus, OH and went to Bainbridge, MD for boot camp.

Memorable experiences include going aboard the USS *Philippine Sea* during shakedown maneuvers in 1946 when the vessel was commissioned and to see new landing operations by a squadron unfamiliar with the aircraft carrier and unfamiliar personnel; participation in the Antarctic Expedition in 1947; encountering the most horrendous storm he would venture to say that any ship ever went through and came out on the other side intact. All of the expansion loops in the power cables and communication cables were snapping like rubber bands where the slack was taken out of them by the stress on the ship and, out of curiosity, he went up and the waves were breaking over the flight deck, which is 125 feet up approximately from the water line. There were many more interesting and exciting experiences but were highlights of his career.

Discharged in April 1948, Charleston NAS, RI. Awards/Medals: WWII Victory Medal. He considers it an honor and a privilege to have served on the USS *Philippine Sea*.

Received training as a plumber/pipe fitter acquiring a journeyman's status, working then for various contractors throughout the state of Ohio, subsequently gained a master plumber's status and operated his own business for approximately 4-1/2 years in southern Ohio. Became a plumber/pipe fitter in the maintenance category for Ford Motor Co. and subsequently General Motors where he served 30 years, retiring in 1990.

Married to Mary almost 50 years at the time of this writing. He has two sons, Michael and Scott.

CHARLES ROBERT (BOB) ARRAS, ADR1, USN RET, born Sept. 24, 1937, St. Louis, MO. Enlisted in the Navy September 1954, attended basic training at NTC Great Lakes, IL.

Assignments: USS *Philippine Sea*, January 1955-December 1956; ATU 213 Chase Field, Beeville, TX, January 1956-February 1960; NS Sangley Point, Republic of the Philippines, March 1960-January 1963; VT-29 NAS Corpus Christi, TX, March 1963-March 1967; NAS Agana, Guam, April 1967-November 1969; VT-31 NAS Corpus Christi, TX, December 1969-April 1974. Retired April 30, 1974.

Married the former Judith Ann Pennington of Refugio, TX. They have four children: Deborah Leigh, Kevin Mark, Susan Michelle, and Loretta Ann. He owns and operates Arras Irrigation and Construction, Corpus Christi, TX.

MARION ALLEN ATWELL, CAPT, born Aug. 20, 1929, Annapolis, MD. BA/MS George Washington University, 1960/1972. NAF Annapolis, July 1947-September 1948; USS *Philippine Sea*, 1948-1951; CNO OP-533, 1951-1954; SupAeroUnitOne, London 1954-1956 AGC, Wx Intell.

Univ. of Minnesota, Project Skyhook, 1956-1958 AGC, Wx Rsrch; USS *John W. Weeks,* 1958-1959, ENS, 1LT, CIC, NAV, OODF; VP-28 1962-1965 LT, NAV/ASW TACCO; USNA, instructor NAV/METRO/OCEANO; VP-28 1968-1969 LCDR, TACTICS; FAW-8 1969-1971 WEPS/ASW; NAVWARCOL 1971-1972 STU; COMFAIRWINGSPAC, 1972-1973 EWO/ASW SP. PROJ; FASU UTAPAO,

Thailand, 1973-1975 CDR OIC; VQ-3 1975-1977 CDR, XO/CO; NRD Denver 1977-1979 CDR, CO; COMNAVBASE; Subic 1979-1981 CDR, PLANS/WEPS/OPS; COMFAIRWESTPAC, Atsugi, Japan 1981-1983 CAPT, ACOS OPS/PLANS; COMUSFAC/COMUSNAVPHIL/USCINCPACREP PHIL 1983-1990 CAPT, ACOS OPS/PLANS/POLMIL/ chief of staff.

Retired July 1, 1990. Medals: LOM, MSM, JSCM, NUC, NCM, MUC, GCM, WWII Victory Medal, CSM, NDSM, KSM, UNSM, KPUC, VSM, AFEM, RVNCM, HSM, NOM, and OSR. He retired July 1, 1990.

Married the former Thusnee Sritanaviboonchi of Bangkok, Thailand. They have three children: Sharon Lou, Allen and Kimberly Arlene.

WILLIAM JOHN ATWELL, SGT, born Sept. 25, 1926, Mt. Carmel, PA. Entered service 1946, Philadelphia, PA; 1948. Reserves until 1950; called back for Korean War. Discharged first time 1948 from Camp Lejeune, NC; second time 1951 from same place. Assignments: Parris Island, Camp Lejeune, NC; Newfoundland, Quantico, VA, and Mediterranean.

As marines, while on Med Cruise, seven of them were in quarters on port side of 5" gun tub. One night as the ship was rolling slightly, a Bearcat fighter that hadn't been tied down rolled off the flight deck, landing on the 5" gun. It crushed the auxiliary fuel tank on belly of the fighter. They smelled high octane fuel and couldn't get out of compartment. The whole crew was mustered because planes captain of maintenance couldn't be found! "Man overboard" alarm was sounded as destroyers zigzagged around area with search lights. A large flight deck wrecker was used to remove plane after hosing it down. Anxious moments, but no one was injured.

Once while watching them change an engine on a Bearcat, a voice behind him said, "Quite an operation isn't it? As he turned around all he saw was gold-it was Admiral Jennings! What a shock and he didn't even salute. The Med Cruise was a remarkable memorable experience.

Awards/Medals: 1943-Served in Merchant Marines and received expert (rifle range) Victory Medal; ribbons for Atlantic Pacific (deck engineer); and Mediterranean on tanker.

Married 47 years to Helen, has five wonderful children and six equally wonderful grandchildren (two already at home with our Lord).

Part-time comb/welder; retired maintenance welder (30 years) for Freestone Tire Oxychemical. Member of American Legion PA Post 0203; POS of A.

VITO A. BALDUCCI, born Feb. 27, 1930, Brooklyn, NY. Enlisted in the USN, New York. Boot camp Great Lakes, IL. Discharged July 12, 1950, San Diego, CA.

Served aboard USS *Philippine Sea* from 1947-1950. Memorable experiences included having a champagne party with his shipmates in France on the *Admiral*.

Awards/Medals: Occupation Service Medal (Europe), Good Conduct Medal.

Married 48 years to Natalie and has four children: Barbara, Cathy, Janine and Robert; and two grandchildren. He enjoys traveling and is enjoying his retirement.

DONALD BARNES, IC1, born June 8, 1933, in Catron, MO. His family moved to Anderson, IN in 1940. He enlisted in the Navy on Jan. 10, 1952 in Indianapolis.

After boot camp he was shipped out to Japan aboard the USS *General Wiegle* to meet the *Philippine Sea*. He was assigned to the E Div. as an IC electrician striker. Later in 1954, he attended IC "A" School in San Diego. He was discharged Jan. 10, 1956.

Attended Ball State Teachers College and worked for Delco Remy in Anderson as an industrial electrical. Retired after 40 years of service. He enjoys fishing, painting, drawing, woodcarving, and traveling both in the United States and overseas. Most recently, he has enjoyed reunions with his Navy buddies.

He married Linda Helvering and they have two children, Torey German and Douglas, and three grandchildren: Hannah and Jenna German and Brianna Barnes.

EARL LEWIS BARNES, A1/c, born Dec. 2, 1930, Gloucester, MA. Entered service Dec. 10, 1947; discharged June 25, 1950, Pensacola, FL.

Assignments: USS *Palau* (CVE-122) Norfolk, VA; USS *Curre*, took detail Philadelphia Navy Yard for ADM Richard Byrd to South Polk; USS *Philippine Sea* (CV-47).

Married Dorothy Adams Sept. 22, 1950 and has six children: Earl Jr., Donna, Robert, Deborah, Scott and Glenn; 11 grandchildren; and four great-grandchildren.

RALPH E. BARNETT, ME2(T), born Jan. 27, 1930, Pittsburgh, PA. Enlisted in the USN April 1948, boot camp Great Lakes, IL. Boarded *Philippine Sea* October 1948 at Quonset Point, RI. Spent four great years on *Philippine Sea*. Most memorable experience was transit of Panama Canal, 1950.

Transferred to USS *Sicily* (CVE), 1952. Discharged April 1953, San Diego, CA.

Worked for Jones & Laughlin Steel Corp. Graham Research Lab as research welder, 1954-1968; 1968-1988 worked for Airco Education Ser. Div. of Airco, Inc. as director of education; 1989-1993 worked at UMAB, Baltimore, MD as construction inspector. Retired 1993 to spend time traveling and continue his activities with Zembo Temple Legion of Honor.

Married Joanne Dietrich, August 1951, San Diego, CA and raised three wonderful children: Deborah, Keith and Stacey. They also have four grandchildren and one great-grandchild.

GEORGE RUSSELL BARR, CPL,
born Feb. 22, 1931, Cambridge, MA. Entered USMC June 8, 1948, Boston, MA; discharged June 7, 1952 USNOTS Inyokern, China Lake, CA.

Assignments: Portsmouth, VA, Sea School; *Philippine Sea*; San Diego Recruit Depot; USN Ordinance Test Station, China Lake, CA.

Enjoyed almost two years aboard *Philippine Sea*, especially the Mediterranean Cruise 1949. Awards/Medals: USMC Good Conduct Medal

Married to Janet Yeo Barr 42 years; she passed away Nov. 1, 1997. He has three children: Cindy, Larry and David, and five grandchildren: Mike, Gregory, Chelsea, Brian, Jason.

Retired 1996 from Bell Atlantic Telephone, 42 years as engineer; doing consulting work for Bell Atlantic three days a week. He enjoys playing golf, boating, and enjoying his grandchildren.

WILLIS C. BEANS, AB3, born Aug. 22, 1928, Pennington, NJ. Inducted July 23, 1947 Philadelphia, PA; boot camp Great Lakes followed by Catapult School. Boarded *Philippine Sea* on Nov. 26, 1947.

Discharged July 3, 1950 at USN Station, San Diego, CA. Medals received were European Occupation and Good Conduct.

Worked 38 years for Amtrak in management and retired as rules examiner in 1993. He has been actively engaged in various activities over the years after Navy. Coaches and manages baseball, football, basketball, also board of directors Hamilton Township Recreation Department 27 years. Nottingham Ambulance Squad 15 years, instructor in senior Red Cross Life Savings, American Heart Association, St. Gregory Holy Name Society, Hamilton Elks Lodge 2262, and active with Deborah Heart and Lung Hospital in Brown Mills, NJ. In his spare time he plays golf, travels, camps, and belongs to a card club.

Married Santa Ann Salvatini in May 1952 and raised seven children: Santa, Grace, William, Barbara, Denneis, Michele and David.

RICHARD W. BOGAR, MM2,
born Sept. 18, 1931, Tacoma, WA. Inducted April 23, 1951, Seattle, WA.; discharged at US NAVREC STA, San Diego, Destroyer Base.

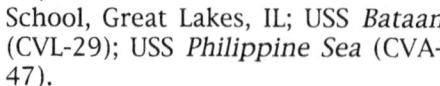

Assignments: USNTC San Diego, CA; Machinist Mate School, Great Lakes, IL; USS *Bataan* (CVL-29); USS *Philippine Sea* (CVA-47).

Memorable experiences: Aft engineer room port H.P. turbine quill shaft failure; low L.O Pressure, stop and lockshaft, operator response excellence.

Awards/Medals: National Defense Service, United Nations Service, Korean Service w/5 stars, China Service, Good Conduct.

Married to Karen E. Campbell 1957; has three children: Richard, Elizabeth, Alice. He enjoys hiking, old motors, shooting, hunting, travel.

RICHARD L. BONIN, PH2, born Dec. 16, 1929 in Attleboro, MA. Joined the Navy in January 1950. Recruit training was at the Great Lakes NTC; followed by Photo School at Pensacola, FL. Shipped out to Yokosuska, Japan aboard the troop ship *General Walker*, December 1950. Boarded the USS *Philippine Sea* at Sasebo, Japan in January 1951. It would be his home until December 1953.

Discharged Dec. 11, 1953. Entered Boston University in February 1954 and graduated in June 1958. Began 32 years of teaching at Norwood Senior High School in Norwood, MA. Received a master's degree in 1963 from Bridgewater State College. Retired in June 1990.

Married to Sandra Harris in 1956 and has five children: Richard L. Bonin Jr., Sandra E. Bonin, Brenda L. Wilkinson, Michael E. Bonin and Timothy J. Bonin. Widowed in 1963. Remarried to Carole Freeman Mendes in 1972. She has two children: Thomas J. Mendes and Kathleen M. St. Pierre. All together they enjoy 13 grandchildren.

WALTER BOUDEWYN BOORSMA, SGT, born Sept. 13, 1934, Minneapolis, MN. Enlisted in USMC July 1953. Boot camp at San Diego MCRD. Sea school March 1954. Summer of 1954 as member of the Sea School Drill Team. Won the West Coast Drill Team championship.

Boarded *Philippine Sea* as MarDet September 1954; transferred to Camp Lejeune July 1955, and to Minneapolis NAS October 1955 as Marine drill instructor until discharge as sergeant November 1958. Earned BA and BS from the University of Minnesota.

Married Gwendolyn Olson in 1957. They raised six children: Daniel, Susan, Thomas, Stephen, Kristen and Jeffery.

Started a construction company in 1960 and continues as general contractor. Some of the more interesting projects were F111 alert facilities at K I Sawyer AFB, and Minot AFB, and Final Assembly Cell, Atomic Energy Commission at Burlington, IA AAP. Looking forward to gradual retirement to spend more time with grandchildren and traveling.

WILLIAM KERMIT BRANAN,
BMCS, USN RET, born May 5, 1929, Stockbridge, GA. Inducted in USN

May 21, 1946, Atlanta, GA; discharged Dec. 27, 1957, Marietta, GA.

Assignments: Recruit training, Bainbridge, MD; NAAS, Chincoteague, VA; NOB, Norfolk, VA; USS *LCS(L)* 65; USS *Philippine Sea* (CV-47); NOB Kwajalein (Sea Bees); NOB Pearl Harbor, T.H.; HASP, Honolulu, T.H.; NAVCRUITSTA, Columbia, SC; SS *Wasp* (CVS-18); COMCARDIV 14; AIRASRON 22, NAVCRUITSTA, Macon, GA.

Was aboard USS *Lake Champlain* when Alan Sheppard was recovered. Awards/Medals: GCM, NOM, CSM, NDSM, WWII Victory Medal, KSM, UNSM and AFEM.

College studies: Fire Science Technology and Criminal Justice. Second career: Fire service, 20 years. Private to Fire Marshall to Fire Chief and Dir. Emerg. Ser.

Married the former Elizabeth Jane Papciak in 1954; has one son, William Mathew. Retired and enjoys camping, trout fishing, and antique vehicle restoration.

ROGER LEE BROKOB, SGT, born Aug. 26, 1934, Lansing, MI. Graduated from Grand Ledge High School in Grand Ledge, MI and immediately enlisted Jan. 27, 1953 in the USMC. Attended boot camp in San Diego, CA. Qualified as expert rifleman at Camp Matthews and was promoted to PFC upon completion of boot camp.

Upon completion of infantry training regiment at Camp Pendleton, Oceanside, CA was transferred to the Recruit Training Center San Diego for Sea School. Reported aboard our *Philippine Sea* anchored off Alameda NAS unloading bombs and ammo preparing to enter dry dock at Hunters Point. Primary duties while a member of gunnery department, 6th Div., the MarDet was the Ships Captains Orderly and assigned to Mount 414 a Quad 40 port side aft. Promoted to Corporal.

Transferred from ship summer of 1955 at Yokosuka, Japan to Camp Lejeune, NC assigned to Fleet Marine Force, 2nd Marine Div., 6th Regt., 3rd Bn., Weapons Co. Attained final rank of sergeant. Released in January 1957. Joined Michigan Bell Telephone Company as a station installer.

Married Katherine Dorris McCrumb in February 1958. In 1961 they were blessed with a son, William Henry Brokob. Retired in 1991 from Ameritech (Mich. Bell) as a telephone engineer. He enjoys grandhildren, golf, hunting, and travel.

BRINFORD REDDING BULLA, entered military Oct. 27, 1943, Newport News, VA. Discharged Jan. 11, 1947, Quonset Point NAS, RI. Assignments: Coast Guard Sta. Airbase, Elizabeth City, NC; NAS, Charleston, RI; NATB, Corpus Christie, TX; NAS, Daytona Beach, FL; NAS, Deland, FL.

After a winter exercise during which they were caught in a snowstorm trying to rendezvous with USS *Yorktown* had to land at Martha's Vineyard in intense snow storm. Searched 63,000 square miles looking for Marine Sqdn. from Ft. Lauderdale, FL during their carrier qualification on converted baby carrier Soloman Islands; stayed out to sea two weeks.

Awards/Medals: Good Conduct Medal and Atlantic Sea Service. He was also the 5th Cadet to graduate with perfect 4.0 in physical fitness test at Corpus Christie in 1945;

Married 50 years to Dorothy Lemon Bulla and has five children; 13 grandchildren; and two great-grandchildren.

Current Activities: Church, travel, walking, swimming, flying, golf, is a Shriner, former president of local postal supervisors branch. Keenly interested in flying, has a valid commercial license, flew with Civil Air Patrol several years.

CHARLES LEO BURNS, LTJG, born July 25, 1923 in Martins Ferry, OH. He enlisted Dec. 14, 1942 in the V-5 Aviation Cadet Program (USNR) in Washington, DC and was called to active duty Oct. 27, 1943 in the Aviation Cadet Program. He trained at RPI in Loudonville, NY; Siena College in Albany, NY; Bunker Hill, IN; Chapel Hill, NC; NAS Pensacola, FL and NAS Opa-Locka, FL.

On April 16, 1946 he was commissioned as an ensign as he received his wings as a naval aviator. He was assigned to Air Group 9 (VF-9A) at Charlestown, RI where he was attached to the USS *Philippine Sea* (CV-47), flying Grumman F8F-1 Bearcats. He reported on Jan. 10, 1947 and served until he was released from active duty on Dec. 20, 1947.

When he came home he joined the reserves at NAS Akron, OH. He was called to active duty Aug. 23, 1950 and reported to VC-11 at NAS San Diego, CA (North Island) on Oct. 13, 1950. He reported to the US Naval Hospital in San Diego, CA where he underwent a brain tumor operation on Jan. 25, 1951 which ended his career. He was officially discharged on April 16, 1952 having attained the rank of Lieutenant Junior Grade USNR.

He marred Mary Snezek on Jan. 15, 1955 and is the father of three children: Thomas, Robert and Kathleen. He is now retired, a widower, and still resides in Martins Ferry.

JAMES L. BURROWS, ETM2, born May 4, 1924, Minneapolis, MN. Entered military July 5, 1946. Died at Merrimack, NH July 7, 1995, leaving his wife of 47 years, Ann, and three children: Jim Jr., Katey and John.

WILBERT E. (BUD) CARIKER, BTG3, born July 29, 1926, Clayton, TX. Entered service first time Jan. 30,

1945, Houston, TX, discharged Aug. 3, 1946, Camp Wallace, Galveston, TX; second time Sept. 13, 1950, Houston, TX.

Assignments: boot camp, San Diego, CA.; Engineer's School, Gulfport, MS; USS *Stoddard* until August 1946; USS *Philippine Sea* 1950-1951. Discharged July 31, 1951, San Francisco, CA. Awards/Medals: Korean Service Medal, Navy Occupation, China Service.

Married Mary Overall and they have two sons, Earnest Allan and Paul Gary. Retired from city of Garland, TX mechanical engineer with the electric power plant July 1991. Deceased Sept. 13, 1993.

CLINTON DEAN CARLYLE,

MM3, born Dec. 23, 1933, Sunnyside, WA. Enlisted January 1952, Spokane, WA. Boarded *Philippine Sea* spring 1952 about halfway through the Korean Conflict. Discharged January 1956, San Diego, CA. His Navy name was "Stick."

He had an emergency appendectomy the day after the Korean Armistice and the doctor must have been good because the ship was riding out a typhoon at the time and his scar is barely visible. Another memorable story was two years after his separation from active duty when he was still in inactive reserves. They had been married almost two months when he received notice that the post office had a registered letter for him and he had to pick it up in person. He was terrified he was being called back to active duty. When he finally picked it up and brought it home, he looked physically ill. Imagine their relief and delight when the "bad news" turned out to be a Navy Unit Commendation, awarded to the ship's crew for service in Korea. Other medals received include the UNSM, KSM w/3 stars, PUC, CSM, NDSM, and GC.

Married Doris Branch September 1957, Asotin, WA and raised three children: Dorinda, Deana and Chad. They have given them eight grandchildren and two great-grandchildren.

Spent 35 years at Potlatch Corporation, Lewiston, ID. Was chosen by Potlatch in 1993 as part of a research task force to help their paper machines advance to the computer age. Retired from Potlatch in June 1994. They still make their home in Clarkston, WA and winter in Yuma where he spends part of his time prospecting.

CHARLES H. CARR, PFC, born April 30, 1928, Mobile, AL. Enlisted in the USMC, July 1947. Boot camp training at Parris Island, followed by Sea School at Portsmouth, VA, then assigned to the *Philippine Sea* MarDet.

Was orderly/driver for executive officer, Cmdr. James M. Peters, Capt. John L. Pratt, and Capt. R.R. Waller. Detached to 2nd Wpns Bn, Camp Lejeune. Transferred to discharged January 1950. Recalled to active duty August 1950 with the 1st 90 mm AAA gun Bn. Discharged July 1951.

Married Geraldine (Jerrie) Oliger July 1949 and they have four children: Deborah, Dennis, Denise and Diane; four grandchildren and one great-granddaughter. Following military service, pursued a career in sales, marketing, and general management.

Since retirement in 1992, activities include local politics, work with special needs children, working and "surfing" the Internet.

BILLY D. CARRELL, E3, born Oct. 7, 1939, Alliance, NE. Entered service July 2, 1957 at Alliance, NE. Assignments: Great Lakes, IL; USS *Philippine Sea*; Moth Ball Fleet, San Diego, CA. Discharged Oct. 2, 1960, San Diego, CA. Awards/Medals: Good Conduct Medal.

WARREN D. CHAPMAN, ABEC, RET, born Oct. 1, 1926, Philadelphia, PA. Enlisted regular Navy July 29, 1944, Philadelphia, PA. Retired Jan. 3, 1963 NAS Moffett Field, CA. Awards/Medals: Usual Campaign plus GC (7) and PUC.

Served on the following ships: Commissioned USS *Orleck* 1945; USS *Marcus Island* (CVE-77) 1945-1946; USS *North Carolina* (BB-55) 1946 decommissioned; USS *Kearsarge* (CV-33) 1947-1948; USS *Saipan* (CVL-48) 1948-1949; USS *Philippine Sea* (CV-47) December 1949-December 1950; V-2 Div. *Barrier* Crew; commissioned USS *Amsterdam*; 1951, Commissioned USS *Point Cruz* (CVE-119), 1952; USS *Point Cruz* (CVE-119) March 1953-1956; USS *Forrestal* (CVA-59); USS *FDR* (CVA-42); commissioned USS *Ranger* (CVA-61) 1957; USS *Midway* (CVA-41 VF-24) 1959-1960; USNA Moffett Field, CA manager CPO Club. Retired January 1963 as CPO.

Since retiring has been in the bar and restaurant business; owned five bars in California, now owns Heights Tavern in Vancouver, WA.

Survived Liberty Launch sinking Hampton Road, VA Memorial Day, 1948; USS *Kearsarge* (CV-33) making chief August 1954; USS *Point Cruz* (CVE-119) Yokosuka, Japan.

Married Anna Elsner 1952 and has four children. Member of Philippine Sea Assoc. plus others.

JOHN M. CHICK SR., RM2, born June 17, 1930 at Gardiner, ME. Enlisted in the USN June 1947 at Augusta, ME. Went through basic training at Great Lakes Naval Training Center. Spent some time at Philadelphia Naval Shipyard, then boarded the *Philippine Sea* (CV-47) in November of 1947, left the *Philippine Sea* in 1950 and spent about a month at Quonset Point, RI before being discharged in April 1950.

Worked for the federal government for many years, first at Portsmouth Naval Shipyard and then for 30 years with the National

Weather Service at Portland and Caribou, ME. Retired in 1985.

Was married to Joyce Whittier for 44 years and raised two sons: John Jr. and Scott. Joyce passed away in 1995 and was married to present wife, Mary Jane, in January of 1998. Since retirement, spend time motorcycling, snowmobiling, fishing, hunting, and many other interests.

CLINTON EARL COOPER, EM2, born Sept. 1, 1928. Inducted in Seattle, WA Aug. 19, 1948; discharged Aug. 13, 1952.

Basic training and Electrician School at San Diego, CA. Traveled to east coast on a destroyer through the Panama Canal up the East Coast to Providence, RI. Boarded the *Philippine Sea* there. When it returned from the Mediterranean Sea returned to the West Coast by way of the Panama Canal and made two trips to Korean area.

He joined the Washington ANG at Geiger Field, Spokane, Sept. 20, 1960. Discharged June 22, 1985. During this time he worked as a technician. Then he joined the Air Force Reserve until Sept. 1, 1988, when he turned 60.

While in the guard he had a 7 level as an electrician, power production specialist, and aircraft mechanic. He worked on F-100s, T-33s, F-102s, and KC-135 refueling tankers as a maintenance mechanic.

While he was in the Washington ANG he was on the rifle and pistol teams from 1966-1977. They traveled all over the United States for competition. He has quite a few trophies.

Has two daughters, Lois and Karen, by previous marriage. Presently married to Myrna for almost 30 years. Has two step-sons, Danny and Curtis. Has a motor home and likes to travel and camp. They belong to the Good Sam's Club and support the Dog's for the Deaf program. Myrna still works and he has his own maintenance business and another part-time job also.

CHESTER D. COPELAND, PH1, born Dec. 5, 1928, Stewart, OH. Entered service on June 18, 1946 at Huntington, WV. Discharged June 6, 1956, Receiving Station, Washington, DC.

Assignments: USS *Philippine Sea* (1949-1950); USS *Boxer* (1950-1951); JCS, Washington, DC; MCB-4 Davisville, RI (1954-1956); NTC Great Lakes (1946); NAS Seattle, WA (1948); NATTC Pensacola, FL (1947); USS *Philippine Sea* (1948-1949); NATCC Pensacola (1949).

Memorable experiences include First Med Cruise (1948); MCB-4 in Pt. Layauty, French Morocco (1954-1955)

Awards/Medals: National Defense Service Medal; Korean Service; United Nations; WWII Victory Medal; Navy Occupation Service Medal (Europe and Asia); Good Conduct Medal; Commendation Letter JCS.

Semi-retired; entrepreneur since 1977. He enjoys hunting and fishing. Married Mary Elizabeth Johnson 1949 (deceased) and has one son, a retired lieutenant colonel, USAF and one grandson.

ROBERT MURRAY CRAIG, RD2, born Nov. 21, 1930, Houston, TX. Joined the Navy Feb. 2, 1949, Houston, TX. Boot camp: USNTS, San Diego, CA (RdSA); attended Radar School at Treasure Island, CA (RdSN); assigned to USS *Suisun* (AVP-53); transferred to USS *Curtiss* (AV-4); attended Radar Countermeasures School, Point Loma, CA; transferred to USS *Philippine Sea* (CV-47), July 1950. Discharged Nov. 13, 1952, USN Rec. Sta., San Diego, CA.

After discharge returned to hometown of Highlands, TX, then moved to Stockton, CA. Earned a BA degree in Zoology from College of Pacific in 1957.

Married Marilyn Joanne Moore of Alameda, CA in June 1954. They have three children. Worked for a year at the Arizona-Sonora Desert Museum in Tucson then moved to University of California at Davis, working in the Poultry Husbandry Department and earning an MS degree in Genetics. While at Davis was active in the Flying Farmers, earning a commercial pilots license and serving on the club's board of directors.

Moved in 1969 back to the Arizona-Sonora Desert Museum at Tucson where he was named general curator until 1977.

Spent a year working for the Navajo Nation in Window Rock, AZ at the Navajo Zoo (1978-1979). Moved the family again in 1979; back to Highlands, TX and worked at various jobs including airport line chief, electrical, and mechanical main-tenance, and computer drafting and design until 1996.

Now retired, spending much time maintaining their cruising houseboat "Sea Urchin," fishing, traveling to reunions, and enjoying nine grandchildren.

RAYMOND L. CRIHFIELD, LCDR, born Jan. 23, 1928, Hillsboro, IL. Enlisted USN April 1946; boot camp, Great Lakes, IL, ETM School, Great Lakes and AETM School, Corpus Christi, TX; reported aboard *Philippine Sea* August 1947; served in V-2 Div., Aviation Electronics Shop; as AT1, transferred NAVTRACEN Memphis March 1950 for instructor duty in TD School.

After making chief, ATC, changed rate to TDC, transferred FAETULANT DET 3, Quonset Point, RI, March 1954; was commissioned ensign (LDO) June 1957, attended NAVCICSCOL, NAS Glynco, GA and then in April 1958 reported to AEWRON ELEVEN (North Atlantic Barrier Sqdn., Patuxent River, MD/Argentia Newfoundland), flew in WV-2 aircraft as airborne CIC officer/air controller, July 1960 transferred AEWRON FOUR (hurricane Hunger

Sqdn., Jacksonville, RL/Roosevelt Roads Puerto Rico) and continued flying in the same capacity. August 1963, attended Electronic Technical Officer's School, NATTC Memphis, upon completion, attended E2-A aircraft electronics system course at Litton Industries, Canoga Park, CA; February 1965 assigned to FCPCP San Diego as E-2A display systems officer.

Awards/Medals: WWII Victory Medal; Navy Occupation Service Medal (Europe); National Defense Service Medal w/bronze star; Good Conduct Medal (3rd); Navy Expeditionary Medal (Cuba); Armed Forces Expeditionary Medal (Cuba), Navy Commendation Medal.

His most memorable experience as a crew member of the *Philippine Sea* took place at Tripoli, Libya. He was dispatched ashore to Wheelus AFB to set up a communications link between the control tower and *Philippine Sea* aircraft. Their aircraft was going to conduct some kind of operation there and there were no standard USAF tower radio frequencies available for Navy use except for emergency frequency. He took a spare aircraft ARC-1 VHF radio, a make-shift antenna, a 24-volt "putt-putt" (gas engine driven generator) and miscellaneous cable and connectors from the ship. He temporarily installed the ARC-1 and the antenna in the upper level of the tower and hoisted the "putt-putt" cable along the outside of the tower up to the ARC-1 location with a line someone appropriated for him. After making some very temporary electrical connections, he started the "putt-putt" and they were on the air!

Retired from USN as LCDR Oct. 31, 1968 then hired as a computer systems engineer at Logicon, Inc. in San Diego; retired from Logicon in 1988.

Married the former Claire M. Ryan of Boston. They have three adult children: Joseph, Cheryl and John. Entire family currently living in the San Diego area.

CLIFFORD C. CROFT III, born July 29, 1930, Dayton, OH. Enlisted in USN 1948; Airman Class "P" school, Memphis, TN. Served on USS *Philippine Sea* during the Korean conflict; discharged April 1953. Medals: UNSM, KSM w/4 stars; CSM, NOSM, Asia Clasp, GCM.

Earned degree in business UCLA. Career in banking; was president and CEO of 5 savings and loans. Started 3 savings and loans, the last being Blue Bonnet Savings Assoc. of Texas.

Former wife, Barbara, deceased; he has two sons, David and John, and one grandson, Dayton. Married, wife Jean Emerton, of England in 1978. They were married 15 years before he died Oct. 9, 1993 after a long illness; buried at Fort Sam Houston National Cemetery with military honors.

He spoke all the time about his years in the Navy, still had his uniform and medals and pictures of the *Philippine Sea*. He was buried with his ship's flight hat "The Philippine Sea."

THOMAS CUNNINGHAM, AB1, born Nov. 9, 1929, Pittsburgh, PA. Entered service on May 1, 1947 in Pittsburgh. Discharged Aug. 17, 1956, Memphis, TN.

Assignments: USS *Curtiss* (AV-4); NAF Annapolis; NAMOTRADET 3001, Memphis. Most memorable experience was Eniwetok bomb tests.

Married to Alice L.; one son, one daughter. Retired Pittsburgh police commander.

DONALD D. DESMOND, AN, born March 15, 1933 at St. Paul, MN. Family moved to Los Angeles, CA in March of 1935. Enlisted in USN Feb. 4, 1952. Following recruit training in San Diego, CA was shipped out to Yokosuka, Japan aboard troop transport USS *General Wiegle* to meet the USS *Philippine Sea* and was assigned to V-1 Div. In January 1953 was transferred to OS Div., then in November 1954 was transferred again to USN Air Station, Brown Field, San Ysidro, CA.

Discharged Jan. 18, 1956, San Diego, CA. Attended El Camino College and California State College at Long Beach studying engineering. Worked for California Division of Transportation, City of Torrance, and City of Simi Valley. Registered civil engineer in the state of California and Arizona.

Memorable experiences include all activities aboard *Philippine Sea*, especially air operations. Awards/Medals: National Defense Service Medal, China Service Medal, Korean Service Medal w/star, United Nations Service Medal, Navy Unit Commendation.

Married Carole Smith, resulting in two children, Jenni Pagano and Dawn Meyer, and three grandchildren: Nichole, Meghan Pagano and Tyler Meyer. Remarried to Carol Divine (Donaldson); three stepchildren: Cheryl Winovitch, Cynthia Kraemer and Carolyn Doyle, and four grand step-children: Courney, John Winovitch, Grant and Derek Kraemer.

Retired in 1992, enjoys painting, travel, golf, and boating at their second home in Lake Havasu, AZ. Member of Masonic Lodge, Sons of Norway Lodge, Business Mens Art Association (past president), Conejo Valley Genealogy Society and American Public Works Association.

ANTHONY DESTEFANO, AB2, born Jan. 5, 1932, New York, NY. Entered service at NATC, San Diego June 21, 1959 and discharged April 20, 1953, NAS Miramar.

Assignments: NATTC, TN; NATTU, PA; NATTU, Severa River; USS *Curtis* (AV-4); USS *Philippine Sea*; Fasron 7 SD; Fasron 7A, FL; NAS Miramar.

Memorable experiences include a discussion with the air boss for firing the port CAT before the pilot was ready.

Awards/Medals: Unit Citation, Good Conduct, China Service, RSM, UNSM, National Defense, HPUC.

Married Jill and they have three children: Anthony, Vincent and Diana. He enjoys fishing, travel, and assisting his wife with her Dressage horse at shows. Retired from AT&T in 1983.

ARTHUR R. DOWNEY, ABCS, born May 15, 1927, San Francisco, CA. Joined United States Merchant Marine, September 1943, sailed until 1951. Enlisted USN Feb. 4, 1952.

Assignments: RTC, NTC San Diego, CA; USS *Philippine Sea* (CV-CVA-CVS-47); USNAS Iwakuni, Japan; USNAS Alameda, CA; USS *Yorktown* (CVS-10); AIRTRANSRON EIGHT Moffett Field, CA; USS *Princeton* (LPH-5); NAVCRUITDIST San Francisco, CA; USS *Enterprise* (CVAN-65. From seaman recruit to senior chief aviation boatswain's mate.

Medals: four GCM, NDSM, UNSM, CSM, KSM, KPUC, NUC, NAM w/combat V device; AFOUA, MUC, VSM, RVCM w/device 1960; RVAFMUC w/Gallantry Cross; APCM, WWII Victory Medal.

Retired USN Sept. 1, 1973 in Washington State. Worked for Gulf Oil in an experimental plant 1974-1980. Worked security NUWES, Keyport, WA from 1981-1989.

Married Linda Ann Curtis of Long Beach, CA at USNS Long Beach, CA Feb. 17, 1969.

Completely retired, moved to Guadalajara, Mexico. Respiratory problems moving back to Washington State. Since returning, his wife Linda graduated from Pacific Lutheran University. She is presently employed by Washington State. He had cataract surgery May 1997 and a quadruple by-pass May 1998. Both were successful and he feels great.

LEO (PAUL) DUVAL, FN, born October 7, 1930, Nashua, NH. He was inducted Feb. 16, 1948 at the Fargo Building, Boston, MA. He served in the USS *Palau* (CVE-122), 1948-1949 and in the USS *Philippine Sea*, 1949-1952.

Memorable experience was going through the Panama Canal in 1950. He was discharged Dec. 5, 1952 at the U.S. RecSta, San Diego, CA. Awards include the Navy Unit Citation, UN Medal, China Service Medal, Korean Service Medal w/3 stars and Navy Occupation Medal.

Married 14 years to Irene. Retired in 1985, part-time building maintenance, and lives in Palm Harbor, FL.

CARL C. DUVALL, PFC, born Oct. 23, 1928, Chanute, KS. Entered service Nov. 9, 1945 in Kansas City, MO; discharged Nov. 8, 1949, 8th & I Marine Barracks, Washington, DC.

Assignments: MCRD, San Diego, CA; *Philippine Sea* (May 1946-May 1947); QPNAS (June 1948); Camp Lejeune & 8th & I (1949); called back 1950 1st Mar. Div., Korea.

Memorable experiences include being wounded May 1, 1947, Quad 40, malfunction. Awards/Medals: Good Conduct, WWII Victory Medal.

Married, three children by first wife; one child by second wife; 13 grandchildren and eight great-grandchildren. Retired operations engineer. He enjoys reunions, fishing, and traveling with companion.

JOSEPH J. DYER SR., RD1(T), born March 21, 1929, Worcester, MA. Enlisted in the USN; boot camp was followed by Radar and CIC School in Boston's Fargo Building. Boarded *Philippine Sea* in November 1948; transferred to USS *Bon Homme Richard*, December 1951; and was discharged March 7, 1952.

Earned degree in chemistry from Clark University. Married Joan Mateo in 1953 and they raised five wonderful children: Debra, Joe Jr., Pat, Tom and John.

Worked 30 years for DuPont Co. and retired as senior process chemist in 1985. During same period he served on the Pennsville, NJ School Board, Town Council as deputy mayor, County Welfare Board (20 years), County Planning Board (five years), the County Commissioner Board (20 years); and as county administrator for three years.

Retired in 1993 to spend his "free" time with the *Philippine Sea* Assoc., Boy Scouts (20 years as scoutmaster and earned Silver Beaver Award), Sportsmen's Club, delivering "Meals on Wheels," his church, six grandchildren and camping in the Jersey Shore Campground.

Served two years as alternate director and is in his ninth year as president of the *Philippine Sea* Assoc.

JACK F. ECK, BMG2/c, born July 23, 1926, Pottstown, PA. Enlisted in the USN Oct. 20, 1944. Took boot camp at the USNTC Sampson, NY.

Commissioned and served on USS *Bagaduce* (ATA-194) during WWII, making calls on Pearl Harbor, Bikini, Eniwetok, Kwajalein, Saipan, Guam, Tinian, Okinawa, and Manila, Leyte, Subic Bay in the Philippines along with ports in China.

Discharged Bainbridge NTC, MD. Joined Navy Reserves in Reading, PA and served as an instructor until recalled to duty during the Korean War and assigned to the staff of Com Fair Jap in Tokyo, Japan. Serving as Adm. G. R. Henderson's boatswain mate.

Transferred to the USS *Philippine Sea* (CV-47), assigned to the 3rd Div.

and ending up in S-2 Div. as mess deck MAA until his transfer to the USS *Windham Bay* for transport to the states for separation from service at TreasureIsland. Medals: ACM, APM, WWII Victory Medal, NDSM, CSM, PLM, NOM, KSM, UNSM.

Worked as a paid driver of the Pottstown Fire Department for 27 years. Now retired and spending all his free time with his wife, Helen.

BRUCE H. EMMONS, CPL, born April 7, 1934 in Sedro-Woolley, WA. Enlisted Oct 1952; reported for active duty Nov 1953; recruit training, MCRD, San Diego, CA (right guide); combat training, Camp Pendleton, CA; Sea School, MCRD, San Diego.

Reported aboard the USS *Philippine Sea* in Hong Kong, October 1954; left the USS *Philippine Sea* in Japan October 1955 released from active duty November 1955, MB/USNS, Treasure Island, CA; discharged July 1961.

Senior planner, Puget Sound Power and Light Co. (38 years); board of directors, North Puget Power Credit Union (27 years); firefighter/EMT-D, Burlington Vol. Fire Dept. (21 years); Advisor/special deputy, Explorer Search and Rescue, Skagit County Sheriff's Office (nine years); City of Burlington Planning Commission (three years).

Interests: Hunting, fishing, black powder shooting, prospecting, and exploring the west from Skagway to the Sonora. Married Donna March 1957 and has three children: Linda, Craig and Eric.

RONALD D. ERICKSON, MM2, born July 15, 1932, Boone, IA. Enlisted USN, boot camp San Diego, CA; MM School Great Lakes, IL. Began *Philippine Sea* duty December 1951, aft engineering room. Discharged May 1955 from Des Base, San Diego.

Department of Water & Power, city of Los Angeles 12 years working from groundman to lineman; 1966 moved to Consumer's Power, Corvallis, OR where he has been for 32 years moving from lineman to foreman to superintendent to chief dispatcher along with an involvement with children through the State Foster Children's Division.

Retirement in early 1998 to travel this great country with his wife, Karen, of 26 years and to spend more time with their children and grandchildren and hopefully to visit some of his *Philippine Sea* buddies.

JOHN F. ESPEN, SN, born March 22, 1930, Bowling Green, OH. Entered USN July 31, 1947; boot camp at Great Lakes Naval Training Center.

Served aboard the USS *Philippine Sea* (CV-47). Memorable experiences include a trip to Arctic Circle in 1948; retired from USPS, 32 years of service.

Discharged Jan. 27, 1950, Quonset Point, RI. Awards/Medals: Navy Occupation Service Medal (Europe).

Married to Wanda; has two daughters: Linda Sattler and Betsy Lundy; six grandchildren and four great-grandchildren. He enjoys mall walking.

JOHN C. (JACK) FANNIN JR., AB2, born April 7, 1932, Philadelphia, PA. Entered military July 1949 NAS, Willow Grove, PA; discharged May 1954 NAS, Alameda, CA.

Assignments: PNSY-NAS, Alameda, CA; USANG New Castle, DE. Memorable experiences include the cold of Korea and Japan.

Awards/Medals: NDSM, UNSM, KSM w/9 stars, KPUC, APCM, CSM, NOM (Asia), NUCM, PUC, NGCM.

Married to Judith McCoy Roller and has four sons, two daughters and 16 grandchildren.

Current Activities: Real estate broker/appraiser (PA), past president DelCo Assoc. Realtors; past Gov. Lions International (DE); commander VFW post 928 (PA); life member VFW ABM Assoc. *Philippine Sea* Assoc.

FRANK B. FIGEL, AOU3, USNR, born Jan. 11, 1935, Mineesville, PA. Entered USNR April 1954, PA. Assignments: PA ANG July 1952-April 1954 with honorable discharge; enlisted USN April 1954, PA; trained at Bainbridge, MD; also stationed in Philadelphia, PA, Norman, OK

Went overseas on to the USS *Philippine Sea* (CV-47) to Korea. Came back 1958, transferred to US NAVRECSTA Navy Base, Philadelphia, PA, the to USN Air Station, Johnville, PA. Honorable Navy discharge July 1960.

Memorable experiences include playing baseball the *Philippine Sea* Wildcats vs. V-5 Div. April 1957 in Korea. Awards/Medals: Good Conduct Medal, Airman School.

Married with two children. Was a tractor-trailer driver, worked for 25 years for Wilson Freight Company, Elizabeth, NJ when he was able.

Had heart problems for 10 years. While on disability taught pitching to Little Leagues, Hasbrour Heights & Hackensack, NJ. Brought in winning teams. Died Sept. 12, 1993 at 58 years old.

ROBERT E. FULLER, RD3, born Oct. 22, 1928, Providence, RI. Enlisted in USNR in 1947 and transferred to USN in 1948; boot camp was followed by Radar School and CIC in Boston's Fargo Building. Boarded USS *Philippine Sea* in June 1949 and served until May 1950 and was discharged from Norfolk, VA.

Married Ellen Guertin in 1953 and raised three wonderful children: Bill, John and Gloria.

Worked in various printing companies in Providence, RI area from discharge to 1959 when started and operated Fuller's Printing Service in Cranston and Hope Valley, RI until June 1991 with his wife, Ellen, for 32 years.

Appointed to tax board of review for town of Hopkinton, RI for five years. Also a member of Chariho Rotary Club and Knights of Columbus.

Retired in 1991 and enjoys gardening, woodworking, and remodeling. Wife, Ellen, passed away from complications of by-pass surgery in 1994.

DAVID L. FULLERTON, AD3, born Sept. 27, 1932, Houston, TX. Entered military July 5, 1950, Houston, TX; boot camp at San Diego, CA. Discharged Sept. 28, 1953, Treasure Island, CA.

Assignments: NRTC, San Diego, CA; USS *Valley Forge* (CV-45); NAS Alameda, CA; USS *Philippine Sea* (CV-47).

Memorable experiences include cruising into Pearl Harbor, cruising under the Golden Gate Bridge. Awards/Medals: GCM, UNSM, NDSM, UCM, Occupation Medal (Asia), KSM.

Married to Rosalie Dement Prevost and raised four children: Michael, Stephen, William and Catherine. He enjoys travel, driving and maintaining a 1940 Ford street rod, working as a piping design draftsman.

JOHN P. (JOCKO) FULLERTON, born Aug. 6, 1930, Big Run, PA. Enlisted USNR Nov. 18, 1947 at Erie, PA. Retired USN Dec. 1, 1969.

Assignments: USS *Albany* (CA-123); AB 'A' School; USS *Philippine Sea* (CV-47); FASRON-4, USS *Hancock* (CVA-19); USNAF Annapolis, MD; USS *Shangri-La* (CVA-38) AEW-3NAS Guam, AEWBARRONPAC BARBERS Pt. Hawaii, VT-9; NAS Meridian, MI; USS *Midway* (CVA-41); VAH-10 NAS Whidbey Island, WA; USS *Constellation* (CVA-64); USS *FDR* (CVA-42); FAETUPAC NAS North Island, CA.

Memorable experiences include being commissioned as LDO in the USN 1962. Working in advertising for the Tacoma News Tribune after retiring from the USN.

Awards/Medals: SNAM, NUC GCM, OCCSM, CSM, NDSM, KSM, AFESM, VNSM, UNSM, KPUC, RVNSM.

Married to the former Ann Stewart Nelson. They have three children and eight grandchildren. Current activities: Enjoying retirement at the Senior Citizens Center!

GENE W. GADD, AB2, born Dec. 15, 1931, Kansas City, MO. Entered military April 10, 1951, San Diego, CA; discharged March 18, 1955, San Diego.

Assignments: USNTC, San Diego, CA; NAS, San Diego; USS *Philippine Sea* (CVA-47).

Worked for Burrough/Welcome Pharmaceutical Company, district manager, 33 years. Retired September 1994. Graduated University of Missouri, Kansas City, business degree.

Memorable experiences include playing varsity baseball and basketball University of Missouri at Kansas City; cubmaster; School Board chairman; president high school booster club.

Awards: *Philippine Sea* baseball and basketball teams (1954-1955); Teams in Navy-NAS, San Diego; basketball (1954-1955).

Married Marianne Turner and they have seven children: Mike, Cathy, Patty, Rebecca, Jeff, Kevin and Brett; also seven grandchildren.

Current activities: high school basketball and baseball coach, Valley Christian High School, Dublin, CA.

ALVIN LLOYD GALLIN, CAPT, born Oct. 14, 1920 in New York City. Graduated USN Academy 1941 with a BS; San Diego State College 1956 with an MA. Served in six destroyers consecutively with one sunk at Guadelcanal and another severely damaged by kamikazes at Okinawa. Gunnery officer *Philippine Sea* January 1958 through decommissioning December 1958.

Other significant duties: commanding *Carpellotti* (APD-136) and *Haleakala* (AE-25); Inspector General MSTS; COMSTS Philippine Islands. After retirement as captain in 1970, became director Maritime Operations Panama Canal.

Among military awards: Legion of Merit w/2 Bronze Stars, Purple Heart, Navy Unit Commendation.

Married Grace Nay Darrough of Rancho Santa Fe, CA 1958. Currently lives in Florida and has a daughter and granddaughter.

CARL L. (LARRY) HANKS, EM3/c, born April 10, 1927, Columbus, OH. Enlisted in the USN Feb. 22, 1945. Following recruit training at Sampson, NY, he was transferred to Bainbridge, MD, NTC, Class A Electricians Mate School, at completion shipped out to Newport, RI Naval Base. Assigned to USS *Philippine Sea* commissioning detail and subsequently to E Division, Interior Communication.

Transferred to USS *Ranger* (CV-4), June 1947, qualifying USN pilots for carrier landings out of Pensacola, FL. Returned to USS *Philippine Sea* October 1947 with decommissioning of USS *Ranger*. Discharged at Quonset Point, RI, then attended Ohio State University, Columbus, OH and University of Illinois at Carbondale. Employed by Battelle Columbus Laboratory, Columbus, OH, 28 years, and McDonnel Douglas, Tittsville, FL, 10 years. Retired April 30, 1982.

Married the former Donna J. Allen of Columbus, OH in 1950. They live in Altamonte Springs, FL and have two daughters, Karen and Stacey, and five grandchildren: Nick, Joe, Lindsey, Steve and Greg.

G. ROBERT HEIKKILA, S2/c, born April 15, 1927, Quincy, MA. Entered military April 1945, Boston; discharged Dec. 5, 1956, USN Rec. Sta., Boston, MA.

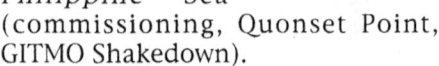

Assignments: Sampson AFB; USS *Randolph*; USS *Philippine Sea* (commissioning, Quonset Point, GITMO Shakedown).

Memorable experiences include photographing all of the airplanes before take off and after.

Married to Sylvia 45 years and is the father of nine children. Retired airline captain for Delta Air Lines. Hobbies: Gardening, photography.

JAMES M. HERR, ME2, born June 18, 1937, Honolulu, HI. Enlisted USN July 26, 1954; boarded *Philippine Sea* right out of boot camp. Left *Philippine Sea* May 1958, Manila Bay; discharged T.I. San Francisco, June 16, 1958. Awards/Medals: Good Conduct.

Memorable experiences include sea snakes while hanging in Bosn chair welding in a new steel plate at sea after collision with another ship.

Worked 27 years at Tektronics, Inc., Beaverton, OR as a model maker. Married and raised four children. Retired 1985. He took up flying in 1978 and went through four planes (no crashes). He now travels a lot in his motor home.

CECIL EDWARD HEWITT, born March 24, 1923, New Marshfield, OH. Enlisted in the Navy Aug. 11, 1941; boot camp at Great Lakes, IL, assigned to USS *Idaho*, served in engine room on USS *Idado* (BB-42), during WWII (October 1941-October 1945).

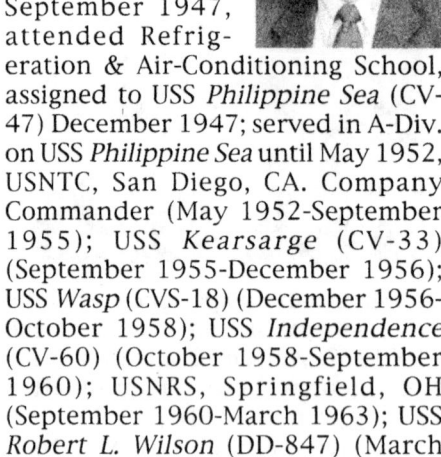

Participated in seven major engagements from the Aleutian Islands to Okinawa.

Re-enlisted September 1947, attended Refrigeration & Air-Conditioning School, assigned to USS *Philippine Sea* (CV-47) December 1947; served in A-Div. on USS *Philippine Sea* until May 1952, USNTC, San Diego, CA. Company Commander (May 1952-September 1955); USS *Kearsarge* (CV-33) (September 1955-December 1956); USS *Wasp* (CVS-18) (December 1956-October 1958); USS *Independence* (CV-60) (October 1958-September 1960); USNRS, Springfield, OH (September 1960-March 1963); USS *Robert L. Wilson* (DD-847) (March 1963-February 1964). Completed courses in mechanical engineering, criminal investigation, steam engineering, and plant management. Retired from USN Feb. 3, 1964.

Medals earned during Navy Service: Good Conduct Medal w/5 stars, 2 Navy Unit Commendations, American Defense Service Medal with "A," American Campaign, European Campaign, Asiatic-Pacific Campaign w/7 stars; WWII Victory Medal; Philippine Liberation; China Service; Armed Services Expeditionary; Navy Occupation; Korean Service; Korean Presidential Unit Citation; United Nations; National Defense.

After retiring from the USN, worked as chief engineer for Horn & Hardart Baking Co., Philadelphia, PA. Plant engineer for Hill Refrigeration, Trenton, NJ; civil engineering superintendent for RCA Service Company, Alaska on the remote radar stations.

Retired in 1985 and resides with his wife, Mary Louise, in Ocala, FL. They have three grown children: Donald Hewitt, SFC, USA (Ret), Sandra Hewitt Truby and John M. Hewitt. Enjoys traveling and going to reunions with his former shipmates. Life member of VFW Post 4209, Ocala, FL and FRA, Branch 179, Gainsville, FL.

HARRY H. HODGES, SN, born May 30, 1935, Smith Mt. Lake, VA. Entered military October 12, 1952, Raleigh, NC; discharged May 1956, Treasure Island, CA. Awards/Medals: Korean Service, National Defense.

Assignments: Boot camp, San Diego; USS *Philippine Sea* (1953-1956); USS *Yorktown* (1956).

Memorable experiences include freezing while on watch on signal bridge during Korean War.

Married Annie and they have one son, one daughter, two grandsons and three granddaughters. Current activities: fur salesman, jogger, works out three-four times a week.

AL D. HORTON, BT3, born June 11, 1937, Marshall, AR. Entered service Dec. 2, 1954, Oklahoma City, OK. Discharged June 11, 1958, Treasure Island, CA.

Assignments: Great Lakes, IL; USS *Philippine Sea* (CV-47). Memorable experiences include visiting foreign countries.

Awards/Medals: Good Conduct, Rifle Marksman, Korean Medal.

Married Trudy and has six children: Steve, Joe, Linda, Mary, David and Robert. Enjoys fishing, camping and traveling in their RV throughout the US.

CLARENCE LEE HOVLAND, CPL, born Jan. 4, 1931, Beloit, WI. Entered service Sept. 20, 1951, Milwaukee, WI. Discharged Sept. 23, 1953, Treasure Island, CA.

Assignments: Boot camp, San Diego; Sea School; USS *Philippine Sea* (1952-1953). Discharged 1953.

Memorable experiences: Japan, made many friends. Awards/Medals: Korean Campaign Ribbon w/4 stars, United Nations and China Service.

Married Janet June 4, 1955 and they have three daughters: Camille, Holly, Dena, four granddaughters and three grandsons. Retired, wintering in Ft. Pierce, FL. Enjoys fishing, grandparenting, traveling.

LAWRENCE A. HOWARD, HM2/c, joined the Navy in September 1942, Lake Charles, LA/Welsh, Louisiana. Boot camp USN Training Center, Chicago, IL. Duty stations were NH Ports, VA, NAS(LTA) Elizabeth City, NC, NTC Sampson, NY (ADMCOM), NABPD San Bruno, Ca, USS *Bell* (DD-587). Discharged from service in early 1946.

Reinlisted May 1946 for two years. Tours of duty on this hitch were USNRS New Orleans, LA, USS *Gordius* (ARL-36), USS *Gyatt* (DD-712), USS *Philippine Sea* (CV-47), and closed out his last remaining time in the service on the USS *Wisconsin* (BB-64).

Attended the University of Southwestern Louisiana for approximately three years and was called back into service for duty at the USNTC, San Diego, CA. Spent the last year and a half of his naval career in the Naval Hospital in San Diego (Pink Prison) and was medically discharged Jan. 1, 1953.

Awards/Medals: Pacific Area Campaign Ribbon, Good Conduct Medal, American Area Campaign Ribbon, Philippine Liberation Ribbon.

Worked as a medical technologist for a group of doctors and remained at this position until he retired in 1985.

He and wife, Janice, have four children and so far eight grandchildren. Retired and grandfathering. On the lighter side, he will be 76 years young in August and can still wear his complete Navy uniform.

ROBERT J. IRWIN, SN1/c, born Jan. 9, 1928 at Grand Rapids, MI. He enlisted in the USN Dec. 27, 1945 which required his father's signature as he was not yet 18. Following enlistment at Grand Rapids he went to the Great Lakes Naval Station at Chicago, IL for boot camp, after which he was assigned to the USS *Philippine Sea* as apprentice, then seaman 2nd and seaman 1st class.

Honorable discharge Oct. 30, 1947. His service included the expedition to the South Pole under the command of ADM Byrd. He was awarded the WWII Victory Medal because he served during the emergency.

Married Janet Bryden in July 1950 and they have six children: Valerie, Wendy, Nancy, Robert, Daniel, and Janet; and 12 grandchildren. He retired from Smith's Industries (formerly Lear, Inc) in 1990 after 35 years.

He enjoys camping, playing upright bass, and gardening. He is a member of the United Methodist Church and a life member of the VFW.

MARVIN WILLIAM JOHANSEN, LCDR, born Jan. 30, 1922, Baltimore, MD. Entered military 1st time Jan. 15, 1943, San Francisco, CA; discharged Jan. 15, 1946, Treasure Island, CA; 2nd time May 1, 1954, San Francisco, CA; discharged June 1, 1956, Treasure Island, CA.

Assignments: Del Monte Preflight, Jacksonville, FL, Deland, FL; Daytona Beach, FL; Alameda, CA; USS *Philippine Sea* A/R Group 9, pilot and LSO (landing signal officer).

Memorable experiences include mid-air collision; another aircraft flew into his. Both landed okay.

Awards/Medals: American Campaign, WWII Victory Medal, Asiatic Pacific Campaign, Korean Service (European & African), National Defense and United Nations Service.

Married Glad and has four children: Eric, Greg, Kris and Susan. Retired and enjoys playing golf twice a week. He is a member of the Civil Air Patrol.

ROBERT T. JOHNSON, RD2, born June 29, 1933, Corbin, KY. Entered military April 8, 1952, Louisville, KY. Military locations include Field Sea. He was discharged April 6, 1956, San Francisco, CA. He is now retired.

CHARLES P. JONES, EMP2, born July 30, 1927, Hudson Falls, NY. Entered military September 1945, Glens Falls, NY; discharged September 1949, San Diego, CA. Re-entered September 1950, NTC Glens Falls, NY; discharged May 1952, San Diego.

Assignments: Great Lakes LC1-789, USS *Washburn* (AKA-108), USS *George D. Liwer* (APA-27), USS *Merrick* (AKA-97), LSTS 1463), Operation of Hi Jump, 1946-1947. After Korea he transferred to the *Philippine Sea* (CV-47).

Awards/Medals: Navy Occupation, Asiatic Pacific Campaign, American Campaign, Korean w/7 stars, Korean Service, Antarctic Service, NUC, Good Conduct, WWII Victory Medal, National Defense, United Nations, China Service.

Has been selling furniture 30 years. MA for Village Hudson Falls, NY (1988-1992). Active 47 years AL Post 574, Commander 1963-1998. Current activities: Volunteer for literacy; volunteer for Big Brothers-Big Sisters Assoc.; Sandy Hill Days.

Have two children: Jeffery and Cheryl, and two granddaughters, Jacey and Jena.

DOUGLAS G. JONES, AB3, born June 20, 1932, Jacksonport, AR. Entered military Oct. 2, 1950, Little Rock, AR; discharged July 14, 1954, Treasure Island, CA.

Assignments: USN boot camp, San Diego, CA; VR-2 NAS Alameda, CA; USS *Philippine Sea*; VR-21, NAS Barbers Point, HI; HASP Honolulu, HI.

Medals: GCM, CSM, NDSM, KSM, UNSM, NOSM, ROKPUC.

Married Eleanor Hahn in 1954. Worked for American Airlines 35 years in Los Angeles, CA and Memphis, TN. He retired in 1991. Now camps, fishes and does some traveling.

EARL LEE JONES, EM1, RET, born April 12, 1939, Tekamah, NE. Entered military May 15, 1956, Boise, ID; discharged Sept. 2, 1975, NAS, Alameda, CA.

Assignments: NRTC, Co 233 San Diego; USS *Philippine Sea* (CVS-47); Naval Support Activity Yokosuka, Japan; USS *Trathen* (DD-530); Naval & Marine Corps Reserve Training Center Denver, CO; USS *Shadwell* (LSD-15); YRBM-20 Vinh Long, RVN; USS *Princeton* (LPH-5) USS *Coral Sea* (CVA-43); FMAG NAS Alameda, CA.

He'll never forget the two west pac tours on the *Philippine Sea*, 30 days looking at dom-dom the rock with 500 marines on board, crossing the equator, the many hours working in the lighting shop, as an electrician and being left behind in the decommissioning crew.

Awards/Medals: Bronze Star Medal w/Combat "V"), Purple Heart Medal, Navy Combat Action Ribbon,, Navy Unit Commendation (two), Good Conduct Medal (three), National Defense Service Medal, Armed Forces Expeditionary Medal, Vietnam Service Medal, Vietnam Gallantry Cross, Vietnam Civil Action Medal and Vietnam Campaign Medal.

Married Marcia Ann Swoboda, Omaha, NE and has four children: Donald, Denise, Earl and William. Retired from civil service and is now customizing a 1950 Chevy. He is a member of the VFW Post 2503, Military Order of the Cootie PT-10, American Legion Post 112, Military Order of the Purple Heart Post 260 and AMVETS Post 25.

RONALD E. KALLAUS, ABU3, born Aug. 19, 1938 in Parsons, KS. Entered military Oct. 1, 1956 at Kansas City, MO; discharged Sept. 30, 1960 from NAS Moffett Field, CA. Received the Good Conduct Medal.

Boot camp at San Diego, CA; then to NAS Norman, OK for A&P School; from there he went to Philadelphia, PA to a school. On Friday, Sept. 13, 1957 he boarded the *Philippine Sea* at Long Beach, CA; left *Philippine Sea* on Dec. 23, 1959 after one cruise. His whole four years was memorable as he was born on a farm and had never been anywhere.

Worked 26 years for Santa Fe Railroad taking an early retirement at 55. Numerous other short time jobs. Now tracing his family tree and at present looking for birth home of his 4th and 5th great-grandparents. Visited the Czech Republic twice and the birth home of his 2nd great-grandparents and birth village of his great-grandfather last year with hopes of returning there soon. From there he has a great story and 850 people in the tree.

Has a son, John, and a daughter, Carole Patrick, with the cutest grandson on earth. Life has been great.

WILLIAM (BILL) L. KERNS, born June 25, 1931 at Rolfe, IA. Entered military Dec. 28, 1950 at Des Moines, IA; discharged October 1954 at Long Beach, CA. Assignments: USS *Philippine Sea* (CVA-47).

He lived on a livestock and grain farm in Iowa for 30 years and retired from the post office with 26 years.

Married Virginia in 1956; they have two children, Kay and Kyle. They are now retired; living in North Central Arkansas, a small town, Midway, AR.

TOMMIE J. KNIGHT, born Nov. 10, 1927 in Vernon, TX. Entered military Aug. 24, 1949, Dallas, TX; discharged March 31, 1953, Seattle, WA.

Assignments: boot camp San Diego, CA; ET School, Treasure Island, CA; *Philippine Sea* (CV-47).

Awards/Medals include the Good Conduct and Meritorious Service Medal.

He and wife Wanda have three sons: Tommy, William and Joe. NASA retired AST electrical engineer.

H. ROSS LaPORTE, AG3, born Nov. 7, 1934 in Biddeford, ME. Boot camp Bainbridge, MD (1952); NATC, Pensacola, FL (1952); NATC Norman, OK (1953); Lakehurst, NJ (1953); USS *Philippine Sea* (1954-1955). For those of you who were on that cruise, he drew the cartoon "Sam SideCleaner" that appeared in the ship's newsletters. Short hitch on USS *Hancock* (mid-1955) until discharged in San Ysidro, CA (Rhem Field) in October 1955.

Worked for the U.S. Weather Bureau at NMC in Suitland, MD; then in Santa Monica, Long Beach, and San Diego, CA. Received bachelor's and master's degrees from San Diego State University. Having done graduate work on remote sensing using NASA satellites, in 1972 helped establish NOAA's new weather satellite (GOES) data distribution program in Washington, DC. In 1982 became the meteorologist-in-charge of the Washington, DC Forecast Center. In 1987 was elevated to a senior executive service position at Weather Service Headquarters as deputy director for the Office of Hydrology. He retired from federal service in 1990.

Married Terry F. Krenach of La Mesa, CA in 1955 and has two children: Ric and Ladona. Now resides at his home on the banks of the Potomac River in Westmoreland County, VA. Lots of boats, some ships, but no aircraft carriers - oh well!

JACK E. LENT, CS2, born Jan. 29, 1930 in Akron, OH. Enlisted in USN; boot camp, San Diego, CA. Boarded

Philippine Sea December 1951. Served three years, seven months and 12 days on the ship, then transferred to North Island Air Station, San Diego.

Discharged Nov. 15, 1955. Medals include the National Defense, Good Conduct, Korean Service w/ star, China Service, United Nations, China Service and Korean Presidential Unit Citation.

Graduated from Barber College. Married Loretta Zverloff in 1950 and they raised four children: Victoria, Rebecca, Carrie and Jack Jr. They have five grandchildren.

Worked 20 years for Fisher Foods, retired bakery manager in 1992. His time spent in retirement includes working for the Veterans of Foreign Wars, held titles of post commander for 14 years, council commander, district commander, where he received all state honors. The Ohio House of Representative 120th General Assembly and Representative Thomas Seese House District #45 presented him with an outstanding Service Recognition Award as the 1993-1994 district 8 commander of the Department of Ohio VFW.

CARROLL L. LEONARD SR., BM3, born Dec. 17, 1931, Lexington, NC. Enlisted USN Seattle, WA in 1950; boot camp followed by assignment USNS Sangley Point, RI. Qualified diver 2nd class, followed by Salvage Diving School, Class 39, Bayonne, NJ.

Returned to Sangley, boarded USS *Mender* ARSD; survey and dive and blow up Japanese prison ship, Oryoku-Maru, sunk Dec. 15, 1944 in Subic Bay by allied aircraft. Over 900 prisoners died out of 1800 on board. Also dived and cut up *Sea Lion,* first sub lost in WWII at Sangley. Assigned *Philippine Sea* 1953; discharged 1954.

Married Dolores Hutchins in December 1950; they reared three wonderful children: Len, Sheri and Robin.

Earned BS in business administration, High Point University and spent 38 years in food business as sales representative and partner in food brokerage business. Sold brokerage and retired in 1992.

IRWIN F. LEWIS, born March 2, 1934, Indianapolis, IN. Enlisted in USMC; boot camp at the MCRD San Diego, CA. Boarded the *Philippine Sea* in March 1954. While on board was a prisoner chaser, captain's orderly, atomic bomb guard and barber. Departed ship in November 1955.

Married Patsy R. Troyer in August 1957 and they have four children: Timothy, Lora, Brian and Daniel, and five grandchildren.

His working career was spent as a barber, welder for Freightliner, Inc. and retired from the Hancock Rural Telephone Company as a lineman.

Both he and his wife retired in 1956 and are enjoying the retirement years traveling and attending the *Philippine Sea* and MarDet reunions and "spoiling" the grandchildren.

CHARLES EARL LONG, FM, born July 14, 1930, Lee County, AL. Enlisted USN at 17 years. Boot camp San Diego NTC. Assigned to FAETU-PAC, Ream Field NAAS, then to San Diego NAS. Transferred to USS *Philippine Sea* July 1, 1950. Service during first Korean Cruise. Discharged Dec. 21, 1951.

Graduated Harris School of Art, Nashville TN in 1958. Worked as advertising artist in San Francisco and Los Angeles. Moved to Huntsville, AL in 1967. Free lance artist until 1990. Today, paints and teaches in watercolor, oil, and pastel and has exhibited art works with American Watercolor Society, Knickerbocker Artist, Disney World Festival of the Masters, National Parts Art Competition, Southern Watercolor Society, and the Georgia and Alabama Watercolor Societies. Also is represented in museum and private collections around the country and overseas.

Married Mary Lou Farrar and they have three children: Vanessa, Eric and Steve.

RALPH M. LUND, SGT, born, June 23, 1929, Brooklyn, NY. Enlisted Feb. 2, 1948, Staten Island, NY; discharged Feb. 2, 1952, China Lake, CA.

Assignments: Parris Island, SC; Sea School, Portsmouth, VA; USS *Philippine Sea* (CV-47), July 1948, Quonset Point, RI; NOTS China Lake, CA.

Married Frances J. Butt in October 1953 in Belmont, MA; they raised two sons, Eric and John. Joined the New York City Fire Department in 1955. Worked in duty stations in Manhattan, Brooklyn and Staten Island. Retired in 1991 after 36 years service.

Retired to Doylestown, PA (1992) in beautiful Bucks County, PA. Has served as church trustee; organized the Marine Detachment of the USS *Philippine Sea* (CV-47); organize and run reunions every two years; has a mailing list of over 200 and sends out quarterly newsletters. Serves as the Marine delegate to the *Philippine Sea* Association. He loves to play golf, travel, garden and play with the grandkids.

DAVID F. LYNCH JR., QM2, born Sept. 9, 1930, Philadelphia, PA. A 1948 graduate of Radnor High School in Wayne, PA, joined the Navy in October of that year and served until September of 1952. Served aboard the *Showboat* from the fall of 1949 through discharge in September 1952 at San Diego, CA.

Assignments: NTC Great Lakes, IL; USS *Siboney* (CVE-112); USS *Philippine Sea* (CV-47). Specialties include ships helmsman (shown in Korean Waters), charts, chronometers and clocks.

Attended Dickinson College then became a career banker with Bryn Mawr Trust, SE National Bank of Pennsylvania and Fidelity Bank N.A. He is now retired.

Father of David F. III and Stephen H. and the grandfather of three. Interests have included Little Theatre, surf fishing and activity in the local American Legion and Sons of the Legion. He resides in Wayne, PA.

RAYMOND A. MARTIN, QM3, born Sept. 23, 1931, Wabash, IN. Graduated Wabash High School (1950). Attended Chicago Technical College (1950-1952). Entered military April 15, 1952, Indianapolis, IN; boot camp at San Diego, CA. Discharged April 13, 1956, San Francisco, CA. Assignments: "N" Div. USS

Philippine Sea, September 1952-April 13, 1956.

Worked for Honeywell, Inc. (1956-1975), engineering department, draftsman/engineer; Markhon, Inc. (1975 to retirement in September 1996), engineering department as a process engineer. Both located in Wabash, IN.

Married Ruth Ann, Dec. 22, 1956; they have three children: Diana Blair, Gary Martin and Linda Sexton; three grandchildren: Randall and Adara Sexton and Todd Blair.

He is a 40-year member American Legion Post 15, Wabash, IN. Served as commander 1965; has held various district five offices and committees. Enjoys attending Purdue University football and basketball games and Wabash Little League baseball.

HARRY A. MATTHEWS III, AM1, born July 1, 1930, Hartford, CT. Entered military June 22, 1948, Springfield, MA; discharged June 21, 1957, USNAS Moffett Field, CA.

Assignments: USNTC, Great Lakes, IL; USNTTC, Memphis, TN; VR-44 NAS Moffett Field, CA; VF-114 NAS North Island, CA; VF-114 USS *Philippine Sea* (CV-47); VF-114 USS *Valley Forge* (CV-45); VF-114 NAS North Island, CA; VR-5 NAS Moffett Field, CA; NAS Alameda, CA; NAS Moffett Field, CA; NAMTD 1086 USNTTC, Memphis, TN; NAMTD 1086 NAS Patuxent River, MD; NAMTD 1086 USNTTC, Memphis, TN; NAMTD 1086 NAS Moffett Field, CA; NAMTD 1086 NAS Miramar, CA; NAMTD 1086 NAS Moffett Field, CA.

Memorable experiences include blind landing on *Philippine Sea* by Ens. E. Jackson VF-112, between wing man and LSO made perfect landing.

Awards/Medals: Good Conduct Medal w/2 stars, Navy Unit Commendation, Occupation Medal w/Asia Clasp, China Service Medal, National Defense Medal, Korea Service Ribbon w/4 stars, UN Medal and Korean Presidential Unit Citation.

Worked 28 years for McDonnell Douglas. Retired as manager contracts administration. During same time period served as commissioner of the Traffic Commission and Parks & Recreation Commission, Torrance, CA. Worked for Magnavox Electronic Systems Co. and retired in 1995 as director contracts management.

Was a widower with two children, Mark Steven and Bonnie. He is now married to former Rita L. Ross.

Retired. He is director of mens' ministries at his church and is a Sunday School teacher.

DONALD RAYMOND McGARRIGLE, LCDR, USN RET, Entered military July 11, 1949, San Bernardino, CA; discharged Nov. 1, 1973, Olathe, KS; Awards/Medals: Purple Heart, Air Medal (7), Navy and Marine Corps Medal, CAR and several medals from Korea and Vietnam Services.

Assignments: COFAT (Saigon); NAS Sangley Pt (Philippines); NAS Olathe, (KS-YP program manager); CAG-9, VF-93 (NAS Alameda); VP-42 (NAS North Island); VRF-32 (NAS North Island).

Memorable experiences include losing an engine (C-47) and making forced landing in Vietnam; loss of brakes and ground looping (C-47) with one wing protruding through an Air Force C-130; carrying wounded and dead South Vietnamese civilians and military under fire.

Married to Brenda D. (Caronna) and has six children, nine grandchildren and two great-grandchildren.

Has his own fund raising company, department manager for builder's service, tax consulting and life/health insurance broker. He flew (as pilot in command) over 5000 hours and 100 hours of combat. He has flown 25 different aircraft and four holds and served on six different ships, BB-62, DD-684, CVA-47, AV-7, AV-12 and AV-13. The aircraft have been single engine, multi-engine, sea planes and land planes.

JAMES L. McINTYRE, AN, born Jan. 23, 1929, Cairo, IL. Entered military July 20, 1950, St. Louis, MO and discharged May 20, 1954, Moffett Field NAS, CA.

Assignments: *Philippine Sea,* five hospitals and Moffett Field NAS, CA.

Memorable experiences included the care he received when he was wounded.

Married to Fern and has two sons, Walt and John, and one grandson, Josh. He enjoys gardening, yard work and going to school basketball games. Worked 37 years with LaClede Steel, Alton, IL and is now retired.

DERRELL G. MILLER, born July 8, 1929, Coalville, UT. Entered military Nov. 3, 1950, Salt Lake City, UT, Fort Douglas and assigned to USS *Philippine Sea* (CVA-47).

Discharged Aug. 14, 1954, San Francisco, CA. Awards include United Nations, Good Conduct, Navy Occupation, China Service and Korean Service.

Married Marilyn and they have four children: Dan, Scott, Mike and Todd. Owner of Utah Communications, 43 years sales and service, two-way radio, radio sites, microwave, CCTV.

ROBERT A. MILLER, born March 31, 1922 in Bay Minette, AL. Enlisted in the USN Oct. 27, 1941 (Navy Day) in Tampa, FL. Went to boot camp in Norfolk, VA. Immediately stationed aboard USS *Yorktown* (CV-5P), sunk during the battle at Midway. Picked up by destroyer. Assigned to USS *Frankford* for convoy duty in the North Atlantic, invasion of Normandy, and Southern France.

Assigned to the USS *Philippine Sea* (CV-47) July 17, 1946 in charge of the forward magazines. Memorable moments were being shaft turns counter; recorder at high speeds; trip to South Pole; watching the launching of R4DS. Navy career included various ships and stations. Aug. 31, 1962 transferred to USN Fleet Reserve. Worked at Polaris Missile Facility Atlantic as a weapons inspector. Served the USN 42 years, 11 months.

Married Madeline Veccia, April 29, 1945; they have two sons, four grandchildren and one great-granddaughter. He and Madeline retired in Ft. Meyers, Fl where they enjoy swimming, boating and are active in the U.S. Power Sqdn. and the Fleet Reserve Association.

DR. LLOYD A. MITTERLING, PHM1/c, born July 22, 1923 in Waterford Mills, IN. Enlisted on Dec. 11, 1941 and was assigned to the USS *YMS-335* pre-commissioning crew on March 10, 1943 at Lake Washington, Seattle, WA. Commissioned on April 9, 1943.

The ship participated in actions in New Guinea, New Britain, Philippines, and Borneo. It was awarded the Navy Unit Commendation at Manila Bay Feb. 14, 1945 and the Presidential Unit Citation at Borneo on June 7, 1945. Also commissioned the USS *Philippine Sea* (CV-47) on May 11, 1946.

He married Cora Hoogenboom Sept. 6, 1946. They have two children. He served with the TBF Squad until discharge in 1947. He attended college on the GI Bill from 1949 to 1954. Taught and did research at Rutgers University. Then, he did research and taught pomology at the University of Connecticut. He has more than 30 scientific and research publications.

Cora passed away in 1974. He retired in 1976 and married Gertrude Hendriksen. He has four stepchildren. Served as president of the Mansfield Lions Club and was an allstate post commander and quartermaster of the Mansfield VFW Post.

RALPH WILLIAM MOORE, born in May in New Windsor, MD and grew up in Manassas, VA. He dropped out of high school and joined the Naval Reserve in April 1945 at the age of 16.

After boot camp at Bainbridge, MD he was sent to NTC, Newport, RI and assigned to the USS *Philippine Sea* (CV-47) for pre-commission training. The ship was commissioned on May 11, 1946 and after several trips to Guantanamo Bay, Cuba, it was assigned to Task Force 68 for "Operation High Jump" to the South Pole. He left the ship on October 20, 1947 for separation from the Navy at Brooklyn Navy Yard, NY.

Married Lois Cornwell, Manassas, VA on Aug. 20, 1949; they have one daughter, Deborah Moore Gentry, Sterling, VA and one grandson, Joshua William Vincill, U.S. Army Band.

Moved to Washington, DC in the spring of 1948 and in July 1951 joined Local 26 of the International Brotherhood of Electrical Workers as an apprentice electrician. After a 39 year career as an electrician in and around Washington, DC he retired in June 1990.

He has volunteered at the USN Memorial since the Heritage Center opened in 1991 and can be found there on most Mondays. He is a charter member of Fort Washington HOG Group and currently serving as historian. He is past master of Camp Springs Lodge #227 AF&AM, past grand inspector of the Grand Lodge of Maryland, and a life member of District Heights Volunteer Fire Department.

SOL NEMAN, CAPT, born Jan. 15, 1919 in New York City. Moved to Temple, TX about 1922. BS EE, University of Texas, 1940. Entered Navy July 1940. Commissioned March 14, 1941 and assigned to USS *Quincy*. Attended USN Postgraduate School 1941-1942. Received certificate in Naval Construction.

Ship superintendent, Charleston Naval Shipyard, 1942-1943. Ship repair facility, Trinidad, 1943-1945. Received MSEE USN Postgraduate School, 1947-1950. Electrical member, Board of Inspection & Survey, Washington, 1950-1953. Chief engineer, *Philippine Sea* 1953-1955. Head, electrical branch, Bureau of Ships 1955-1960.

Promoted to Captain 1960. Philadelphia Naval Shipyard 1960-1960.; Asst. fleet maintenance officer, staff COMSERVPAC & CINCPACFLT 1963-1967. Retired July 1967.

Employed at Lockheed, Electrical Design, DSRV naval rescue submarine 1967-1969. Returned to Temple 1969. President Temple Iron & Metal Co./Temple Steel Service/Industrial Container Service, 1970-1989.

JOHN JOSEPH NOGA, S2/c, RD (Striker), born March 28, 1927, Millers Falls, MA. Enlisted Dec. 29, 1944; boot camp NTC, Sampson, NY; Radar Group School at Cavalier Hotel, Virginia Beach, VA; CIC Group Training Center (Fargo Building), Boston, MA.

Boarded *Philippine Sea* 1945 South Boston Dry Dock, Boston, MA. Original crew member in the commissioning of the USS *Philippine Sea* (CV-47) on May 11, 1946. Capt. Delbert S. Cornwell, USN, took command of the Navy's "newest man of war." Sailed June 13, 1946 for NAS Quonset Point, RI. War in Pacific was ending allowing early discharge July 31, 1946. S/Sgt. USAF during Korean War. 6007th Medical Sqdn., Tokyo, Japan (1949-1953). Unable for time off to visit *Philippine Sea* when in various ports.

Worked 33 years for old New England Telephone & Telegraph. Retired in 1988.

Married Marie A. Powers Sept. 7, 1957; they have two wonderful daughters, Martha and Anne, and one granddaughter, Elizabeth Ashley.

ALFRED NOVACEK, AN, AK-Striker, born June 15, 1935, Dwight, NC. Entered Navy December 26, 1956, Lincoln Naval Reserve Station, Lincoln, NE; discharged February 27, 1959, North Island, San Diego, CA.

Assignments: North Island; VS-21; *Philippine Sea*. Memorable experiences include 1968 West Pac; crossing equator; search for airliner, Oceanlink.

Married Yvonne Liska; two sons, Trevor and Todd Walsh (one grandson).

Semi-retired. Owned and operated retail grain elevator and building supply company. Was village clerk for 35 years and active in civic affairs.

EDWARD EUGENE NUGENT, born Aug. 28, 1931, Leavenworth, WA. Retired as a chief cryptologic technician and linquist after changing rate as a first class aviation boatswain mate. Subsequent to transfer from *Philippine Sea* served VR-5, CVE-86, and 92, crash crew then beachmaster Pensacola area, LPO boxer Hangerdeck and MAA on *Shangri-La*. Other duties included Turkey, Cyprus, Cuba, and Washington, DC.

After Navy retirement in 1969 earned BAs in political science and social work. Community involvement included serving as president Kiwanis, Civitan, Cancer Society, and chairman of the county Republican Executive Committee.

Married the former Rebekah F. Huff in 1956. They have three children: Cheryl, Ed Jr. and Sandi. Sandi has two children, Amber Rae and Tamara Rebekah.

The past nine years of retirement he and Becky have been volunteers at the National Museum of Naval Aviation in Pensacola; Becky at the Information Desk and he as tour guide and occasional writer for the magazine *Foundation*.

VIRGIL D. ODGERS, CS3, born July 31, 1929 in Colorado Springs, CO. Enlisted in the Navy July 19, 1948 in Denver, CO. Went to boot camp and commissary school in San Diego. Spent 2-1/2 years on NOB Guam. Medals: Good Conduct, UN, Korean War.

Boarded the *Philippine Sea* in July 1951 until discharge on July 9, 1952, moved to Los Angeles and worked for all the major aircraft companies. Retired Dec. 1, 1989, became active in St. John Lutheran Church and Southern California Lutheran Cursillo.

He enjoys retirement and travel when possible.

DONALD W. PARONI, AM2, born July 20, 1930, Chicago, IL. Entered military April 1951, downtown Chicago, IL; discharged 1955 in San Diego, CA.

Assignments at Millington AFB, Memphis, TN; Jacksonville FASRON-8, Alameda, CA. Memorable exper-ience was living 20 years in four years.

A widower, he remarried (21 years) and has six children and 12 grandchildren.

He enjoys singing, pitching horseshoes, shooting pool and has fun traveling, Las Vegas, Laughlin.

RICHARD D. PETERSON, AB3, born May 8, 1934. Entered Navy June 2, 1952 at Great Lakes, IL. Assignments: NAS Whidbey Island, WA; USS *Philippine Sea* December 1952-December 1954; NAS San Diego December 1954-June 1956.

Memorable experiences include being a member of V2C championship basketball team. Discharged June 2, 1956, San Diego, CA. Awards include the National Defense, UN, Korea Service, China Service, Good Conduct and Navy Unit Citation.

Married Dorothy Malliet in December of 1954; they raised two children, Judy and David.

Retired as manager of Automotive Operations for Ameri-tech; wife is retired school teacher. He is enjoying retirement on Eagle River chain of 14 lakes in northern Wisconsin.

JAMES RAY PITTMAN, FN2/c, born July 31, 1927, Goldsboro, NC. Entered military June 19, 1946 with assignments on aircraft carriers. Boot camp was at Bainbridge, MD; went from Raleigh, NC to USS *Philippine Sea*, Providence, RI; to USS *Kearsarge* (CV-33), Brooklyn, NY.

Memorable experiences include ADM R.E. Byrd's expedition to the South Pole in 1947 going through the Panama Canal and across International Date Line watched as three DC 3 aircraft took off of *Philippine Sea* flight deck. Discharged March 26, 1948, Receiving Station, Brooklyn, NY.

Married to Anne Boyette September 10, 1949 and will celebrate 50 years of marriage in 1999. They have one daughter, a son-in-law and two grandchildren, Sarah and Tim.

Retired and doing lots of reading.

RONALD JAMES PLOWE, born Dec. 12, 1927, Hancock, MI. Inducted Jan. 8, 1946; Great Lakes Training Center Co. 7; boarded *Philippine Sea* in Boston dry dock for shakedown cruise to Cuba. Quartermaster School Newport, RI; Operation High Jump to South Pole expert rifleman. Discharged Nov. 7, 1947.

Attended Mighican State College 2-1/2 years. Graduated Wisconsin Institute of Mortuary Science. Owned and operated Plowe Funeral Home in Ludington, MI 10 years. Owned and operated Ventura Motel in Ludington, MI for nine years.

Currently painting and selling figurines made of pecan shells at craft shows nationwide. Hobbies are scuba diving, metal detecting and writing poetry and articles for magazines and newspapers.

WILLIAM JAMES POE, SSgt, USMC, born March 10, 1928, Melvindale, MI. Enlisted July 1945. Boarded *Philippine Sea* in August 1946 at Quonset Point, RI. After leaving the *Philippine Sea* November 1947, inspector/instructor staff, Detroit, MI, Recruiters School, 1951. Assigned duty at Detroit, MI.

He was discharged from USMC in November 1954. Medals include the GCM and WWII Victory Medal.

His entire career with the USMC was exciting. The most memorable was crossing the equator and becoming a member of the "Order of the Penguin" when the *Philippine Sea* crossed the Antarctic Circle Jan. 24, 1947.

Married the former Mary McCreery on March 22, 1996. (She was his first love in school when they were kids!) Retired from Kalama Chemical, Inc. 1983. Both he and Mary love to travel and just enjoy life.

THOMAS C. POLLARD, S1/c, born March 31, 1928, New Bedford, MA. Enlisted Nov. 7, 1945, Boston, MA. Assignments: US NTC Bainbridge, MD; USN Advanced Base, Weser River Bremerhaven, Germany; USS *Leyte* (CV-32); USS *Philippine Sea* (CV-47).

Discharged Oct. 13, 1947, Brooklyn, NY. Awards/Medals: WWII Victory Medal, WWII Naval Occupation and American Area Campaign.

Married to former Priscilla A. Bender; she passed away in 1988. He has three daughters: Cynthia, Joyce and Betty. Retired from banking in 1995. He is a past commander VFW Post 6643, Freetown, MA.

JUNIOR R. PRICE, MSGT, USMC, born April 19, 1925, N. Creagerstown, MD. Entered military Dec. 5, 1945, Syracuse, NY; discharged July 31, 1968, Philadelphia, PA. Awards/Medals: Good Conduct Medal, 7th Award, Korean Service Medal, Vietnam Service Medal.

Assignments: USS *Philippine Sea* May 1946-Aug. 1949; MB NY Naval Shipyard 1949-1952; AT Co. 1st Mar. 1952-1953; MB Camp Lejeune Base Prop 1953-958; 1&1 duty New Castle, PA 1958-1961; 1st Bn March 1961-1962; 1&1 duty Altoona, PA 1964-1966; 3rd MAF Vietnam 1966-1967; DOS Philadelphia, PA 1967-1968.

Memorable experiences include Operation High Jump, *Philippine Sea* 1942, European Deployment 1948-1949.

Married Lora Sue Bock Jan. 5, 1957; they have four children: Ralph, Brian, Bronwen and Sally.

Has worked as custodian of the Church of Jesus Christ of Latter Day Saints since Jan. 20, 1969.

DONALD LEE PROCTOR, born Aug. 4, 1929 in Akron, OH. Deceased Sept. 22, 1990. Enlisted in the USMC August 15, 1949; boot camp Parris Island, attended Demolition School, consequently served on the USS *Philippine Sea* from May 24, 1950-Dec. 15, 1951.

He was discharged Nov. 28, 1952. Awards/Medals: Navy Occupation, Korean Service w/5 stars, China Service, Purple Heart, United Nations, Presidential Unit Citation, Letter Commendation, Command FarPac FMF.

Worked for the Teamsters from 1959-1971 and the operating engineers from 1971-1990.

He had four children from his first marriage: Donna, Matthew, Kathleen and Lisa. Remarried in 1973 to Pauline Vasiliou, married for 17 years until his death.

He was an avid reader of American history and the American Indians. He had several hobbies, one of which as painting. His great love however, was building and flying radio controlled airplanes. He was a man who thoroughly enjoyed his life and brought much happiness and laughter to his family and to all who knew him. His memory remains eternal.

LOUIS S. PROK JR., born May 29, 1928. Entered military December 26, 1945, New York City; Assignments: BB-55 USS *North Carolina*, Fire Fighting School three weeks, 5-inch Dam Neck, VA two weeks, USS *Philippine Sea* (CV-47).

Discharged Quonset Point, RI June 1, 1949. Awards/Medals: European Occupation, Order of Penguin, WWII Victory Medal, Good Conduct Medal, American Theatre.

Retired after 41 years at AKZO Nobel. He is a member of the American Legion.

H. FLINT RANNEY, LT, USNR, RET, born March 26, 1935, Orange, NJ. BA at Dartmouth College, 1956. NROTC Regular Midshipman from 1953-1956. Commissioned ensign, USN, June 1956; promoted to LTJG, September 1957.

He was 5th Div. officer on USS *Philippine Sea* (CVS-47), September 1956-December 1958; decommissioned ship at Long Beach Naval Shipyard; assigned as F Div. officer on USS *Ranger* (CV-61), December 1958-September 1959; inactive Naval Reserve until 1962, honorable discharge as lieutenant.

Memorable experiences include Operation OceanLink 1958; decommissioning *Philippine Sea*, December 1958; Cruise Book Editor.

He worked in the sound recording business, as a stock broker, and since 1978 as a real estate broker on Nantucket Island, MA. He was elected to the Nantucket School Committee for nine years and the School Building Committee for four years. He is past president of the Chamber of Commerce, and is treasurer of the Rotary Club.

Married the former Charron (Corky) McPherson of Stratford, Ontario, Canada, in 1965. They live on Nantucket and have five energetic children of whom the youngest is another Ensign Ranney, a Citadel graduate and a qualified Navy diver serving on the rescue ship USS *Safeguard* (ARS-50) in Pearl Harbor. They also have three grandchildren.

RONALD V. RAY, F1/c, born Dec. 20, 1928, McConnelsville, OH. Entered military Dec. 26, 1945, Columbus, OH; Assignments: NTC Great Lakes, IL, Newport, RI, USS *Philippine Sea* (CV-47).

Memorable experiences include ships commissioning in May 1946, ADM Byrd's expedition, Operation High Jump, Crossing Equator and Antarctic Circle.

Discharged Oct. 30, 1947, Brooklyn, NY. Awards/Medals: WWII Victory Medal and Antarctica Service Medal.

Married Mary E. Johnson June 26, 1946; they have four children: Ronald, Cheryl, John and Steven Tracey (Deceased). Retired 1994, owned and operated auto body shop 47 years; Bristol Twp. trustee 32 years; Masonic Lodge 40 years; American Legion 23 years; has two show cars, 1956 Mercury and 1960 Lincoln, and attends local festivals and car meets.

JOSEPH V. RECA, IC1, born Jan. 31, 1924, Philadelphia, PA. Enlisted in the USN April 1943; boot camp at Bainbridge, MD followed by IC School at Anacostia, Washington, DC. Commissioned the USS *Stormes* (DD-780) at Bremerton, WA, and served in the Pacific. Transferred to USS *Roosevelt* (CVB-42) April 1, 1946; to USS *Sicily* (CVE-118 May 27, 1947; to USS *Philippine Sea* (CV-47) Nov. 28, 1947.

Left *Philippine Sea* March 16, 1949 and discharged at Norfolk, VA April 13, 1949. Medals include Asiatic-Pacific Area, American Area, Victory Medal, Navy Occupation Service Medal and Good Conduct Medal.

Degree in electrical engineering from Drexel University, Philadelphia, PA and a law degree from University of Baltimore, MD. Worked 34-1/2 years at Westinghouse Electric Corp., Baltimore, MD; retired 1989.

Married the former Alice Lee Holzbach of Richmond, VA. Has three sons: Robert, Joe Jr., and Timothy; three granddaughters: Andrea, Hannah and Maggie with another grandchild due in October 1998.

JACK F. RHODES, SGT, born March 11, 1931, Muskegon, MI. Enlisted USMC; boot camp Parris Island. Stationed at Parris Island as rifle coach and played football. Went to Sea School Portsmouth, VA. Boarded *Philippine Sea* June 1952, came back to states on the *Valley Forge*. Assigned to 2nd Marine Div. Camp Lejeune, NC.

Discharged Dec. 19, 1952 as Sergeant, Infantry Unit Leader. Medals include Navy Occupation, Korean Service w/5 stars, China Service, United Nations Ribbon and Good Conduct Medal.

Married Janice Chavez from San Francisco, CA; they have seven children: Nancy, Cathy, Sonja, Susan, Jeffery, Joann and Aimee.

Worked in construction administration from 1953-1974 at which time he started his own business. Retired in 1990. They are now living the good life.

WILLIAM L. RIES, AE3, born Aug. 16, 1934, Massillon, OH. Enlisted in Navy Reserve Dec. 16, 1952, NAS Akron, OH; active duty April 11, 1957, Philadelphia, PA.

Assignments: USNR Air Station, Akron, OH, VS-653, NAS Philadelphia, PA, USS *Philippine Sea*, USS *Kearsarge* (CVS-33)

Memorable experiences: When he arrived on the *Philippine Sea* part of his records were lost (where he was transferred from MMLFN to AN) so he was placed in No. 4 boiler room till the rest of records came and he was transferred to the air department and the flight deck (cool fresh air at last).

Released to inactive duty in USNR, USS *Kearsarge* (CVS-33) at Long Beach, CA. Honorable discharge from USNR Dec. 16, 1960. Awards/Medals: Good Conduct Medal (2nd Award).

Earned pilot license, worked for Eaton Corp. 41 years. Retired 1995 as senior maintenance person to spend free time boating, flying and dealing guns.

Married Barbara Donvon of Massillon; they have two children, William and Mary.

EARL L. ROGERS, SN, born Feb. 16, 1931, Fort Dodge, IA. Enlisted in the USN September 1950; boot camp at Great Lakes, IL. Sent to California. Boarded the SS *Pine Island* 2nd Div. Transferred to the USS *Philippine Sea* OR Div. in 1951. After three cruises on the *Philippine Sea* was transferred to North Island in Fasron 110; discharged July 1954.

Married Glenna Venable Oct. 13, 1952. Had three children: Douglas, Denise and Daniel. Dan was killed in a car wreck June 1986. They have five grandsons and one granddaughter. Owned and operated Roger's DX service station until legal blindness forced retirement.

NORMAN L. ROSEN, MMR3, born March 21, 1927 in Des Moines, IA. Enlisted in Navy in 1945. He served with the Seabees in the Philippine Islands and was recalled June 1951 to serve on board the *Philippine Sea*.

He arrived at Hunters Point, went aboard in June 1951 and attached to "A" Div. Spent time aboard keeping engineers' store room. Stood watch in after steering. The job was to purge air out of steering cylinders.

Memorable experiences were just being aboard, seeing snow on flight deck. Was discharged in San Diego in September 1952.

He married Nancy Kjeer in 1952 and they raised two children. They also have five grandchildren and one great-grandchild. Worked 34 years at National Gypsum Company in Fort Dodge, IA as purchasing agent. He taught Sunday School, sang in church choir, and served on various church committees. Sang with Fort Dodge Glee Club. Retired in 1989 and is enjoying his grandchildren.

RICHARD D. ROSENBERRY, AE1, born Dec. 6, 1931, Garrett, IN. Entered military June 13, 1949, Indianapolis, IN. Assignments: NAS Memphis (A School); NAS North Island (VF-113), USS *Philippine Sea* (VF-113, CAG-11, 1950, 1951, 1952); NAS Mirimar (VF-113) NAS Los Alimitos (USNR-R, VP-773).

Discharged April 7, 1952, San Diego, CA; 1970 NAS Los Alimitos (USNR-R).Awards/Medals: GCM, KSM, UNSM, CSM, JOM, NRM, ADM, ASW Aircrew.

Worked 37 years with Department of Defense as an aircraft electrical specialist for 16 years and as a quality assurance specialist for the Defense Contract Administration Services for 17 years. Worked on all the Apollo missions up to Apollo-13 and the Lunar Landing and Space Lab.

Married high school sweetheart Ilene Lou O'Brien; they have seven children, 10 grandchildren and five great-grandchildren.

Retired Dec. 13, 1987 and enjoys traveling, flying Ultra-Lite aircraft, fishing.

CARL FRANCIS SANFORD, SK2, USN, born March 24, 1928 in Margaretville, NY. Enlisted March 31, 1948. Following recruit training in Naval Training Center, Great Lakes, IL was shipped to Bayone, NJ for store keeping training then to the USS *Philippine Sea* (CV-47)

Assignments: Fleet Aircraft Services, Sqdn. Four, NAS San Diego, Korea Service Medal w/3 Bronze Stars, China Service Medal, Navy Occupation Medal w/Asia Clasp, UN Service Medal w/2 ribbons, Recommended for Good Conduct Medal. Honorable discharge March 30, 1953 from San Diego, CA, North Island.

Memorable experiences include being in the North Atlantic, watching air craft land, take-off and battle station by 5" guns.

Married Margaret Gladys Owen, July 21, 1951; they have two sons: Douglas Wayne and Wesley Guy; five grandchildren: Kimberly Rose, Douglas Wayne, Daniel Wesley, David Winfield, and Derek Whitney.

Drove Hess Oil tractor trailer for 25 years. Retired and enjoys camping, traveling, antique cars, church, and holding services in nursing homes.

DANIEL J. SAWYER, RD2, born Oct. 11, 1927, Benington, VT. Entered USN Sept. 7, 1945 in Albany, NY. Assignments: USNTC, Great Lakes, IL; RDM School, Point Loma, San Diego, CA; Radar, CIC School, Fargo Building, Boston, MA; USNTS, Newport, RI; USS *Philippine Sea* (CV-47), plankowner, May 20, 1946-Oct. 7, 1948.

Memorable experiences include: three Caribbean tours; Mediterranean tour 1948; Antarctic Expedition, Operation High Jump (1946-1947); traversing Panama Canal; bridge contact with ADM Richard E. Byrd (January 1947); 50th annual reunion, Operation High Jump, Norfolk, VA (October 1996).

Discharged Oct. 7, 1948, NAS Quonset Point, RI. Awards/Medals: WWIIVM, GCM, Navy "E", HSLB, HDB, OSM (Europe), Antarctic Expeditionary Medal, Order of the Penguins, RDM School, Advanced Carrier CIC Training and Ancient Order of the Deep.

Married to Mary W. Wolchek August 1952, Bennington, VT; they have three sons: Paul, Mark and Peter.

BS degree, Springfield College, MA, 1953; Advanced, Cornell University, Potsdam State, Thiel, Onentia State, Siena, Albany State; 36 years of continuous teaching (1953-1989) at Fort Plain, Fleischmanns and Averill Park, NY; member of NYSOT, AFT, APCS Associations; American Legion, American Polar Society, Operation High Jump Assoc., NYS Retired Teachers, St. Henry's Church and USN Memorial Foundation.

Current activities: 1989, retired from Averill Park Central School, Averill Park, NY; joined USS *Philippine Sea* (CV-47) Assoc. He enjoys travel, tennis, golf, and family.

JOSEPH J. SIDLO, EMP3, born Jan. 14, 1930, Chicago, IL. Enlisted in USNR April 1947, Chicago, IL. Served actively in USNR Surface Div. 9-4, Chicago, IL. Called to active duty during the Korean War in September 1950. Served aboard the USS *Philippine Sea* (CV-47) until 1951.

Received honorable discharge Dec. 21, 1951, at San Diego, CA (destroyer base). Awards include the

KSM, UNSM, CSM, NUC and Korean PUC.

Married Audrey Kavale May 1956 and raised two children, Janet and David. They have four grandchildren. Attended the University of Illinois, Chicago and the Illinois Institute of Technology. Pursued a 25-year engineering career with major Chicago corporations, including Sunbeam and Bell & Howell, in Consumer Product Design & Development.

Left corporate life in 1977 to establish own commercial printing business, Pace Printing, Inc., Arlington Heights, IL.

Son David will assume full control of business in 1999. He and his wife will try retirement, concentrating on family, travel and church.

EDGAR A. SIEWERT, IC3, born Nov. 9, 1927, Slayton, MN. Enlisted in the USN October 1945; boot camp San Diego, Electricians School Great Lakes, and boarded *Philippine Sea* May 1946-1948 when discharged as intercommunication electrician 3rd class. Awards include NGC, ACM, WWII VM, Navy Occupation and Antarctic Service.

Enlisted in MNARNG January 1949 while attending college and received pilot and aircraft mechanics license. Activated in January 1951-September 1952 as tank commander. Worked as aircraft electrician for several years. Enlisted in OKARNG May 1961 as tank gunner in Claremore, OK. Started work full time for the unit November 1961 as administrative supply technician.

Transferred to Tulsa, OK in August 1972 as operation training & readiness spec (E-8). Transferred to HHD OKARNG, Oklahoma City August 1976 as state command sergeant major (E-9) working in the operations & training department. January 1978 assigned as command sergeant major of training site det. April 1980 assigned as commandant of OKARNG NCO School. August 1982 assigned as chief operation sergeant in HQ STARC until he retired in November 1987.

Called back to active duty February 1991-May to man a family support center in Oklahoma City for Desert Storm. Now working with rental property and volunteering.

Married Irene and has son, Kevin; two grandsons and one great-granddaughter.

ROBERT A. SMITH JR., born Oct. 15, 1929, Tennille, GA. Enlisted in USN 1948; boot camp San Diego, then to Radio School and assigned temporary duty Naval War College, Newport, RI, until the *Philippine Sea* returned from duty in the Mediterranean. Stationed on the *Philippine Sea* until June 1952.

Left the ship in Yokosuka and took a slow boat back to San Francisco for discharge July 1952 at Treasure Island. Attended University of Georgia, pre-engineering, STI, degree mechanical engineer tech, AAU, degree BBA.

Worked with Savannah Gas Company and Atlanta Gas Light Company division superintendent and manager propane operation for 35 years. Retired 1992. Moved to Columbia, SC to be closer to son, Robert; daughter, Lisa; and grandchildren, Ethan and Jared.

LEE H. SNYDER, born Sept. 23, 1927, Fulton, MI and grew up on a farm. Upon discharge in 1948 he went to work for General Foods Corporation, Post Div. Left in 1958 (was assistant planning manager). Entered USNR Sept. 20, 1945 in Detroit, MI.

Assignments: USNRS, Detroit, MI; NTC, Great Lakes, IL; USN PerSepCen, Great Lakes, IL; R/S Brooklyn, NY; USS *Philippine Sea* (CV-47). Memorable experiences include Task Force 68, Operation High Jump, 1946-1947 Navy South Pole Expedition, Mediterranean Cruise February 1948-June 1948.

Awards/Medals: OSR, GCM, WWIIVM, ATM, Honorable Service Lapel Button, Honorable Discharge Button. Discharged Sept. 23, 1948, PDSA NAS Quonset Point, RI.

Earned BS in industrial supervision at Western Michigan University in 1962. Earned degree from Indiana University in traffic and transportation in 1970. Worked for Hoover Ball Bearing from 1962-1967 as shipping and receiving supervisor in Ann Arbor, MI. Worked 1968-1975 for St. Regis Paper Company as distribution manager. Designed warehouses, installed systems, and computerized the shipping, receiving departments at various sites in the country. This continued with other companies until 1980.

From 1980 to retirement in 1989 worked for Hughes Aircraft Company in California. Responsible for division's inventory valued at $50,000,000. Wrote systems and computerized the receiving and shipping areas. Supervised 24 people in this operation at five locations.

Never married. He has done lots of volunteer work since retirement. This involves the IRS from January-April 15, also volunteer work for Lake County Sheriff's Department, his church (both 1/2 day per week) and this involves data input. He plays tennis, golf, and Pinochle on a regular basis.

ARTHUR R. STAHL, PFC, born April 14, 1928, Minneapolis, MN. Enlisted USMC on Nov. 7, 1945 at Hollywood, CA; discharged Nov. 6, 1948 at Camp Pendleton, CA.

Assignments: USMCRD & Sea School, San Diego, CA; USS *Philippine Sea*; 2nd & 6th Marine Divs. Memorable experiences include being RAdm R.E. Byrd's orderly on 5th Antarctic Expedition.

Married the former Jeannine M. Cash in November 1956. Spent 20+ years with MacWhyte Wire Rope Co., resigned as national sales manager, moved to the southwest, owned and operated Artweld Co. Now retired.

JOHN LAWRENCE STEELE, ADAN, born June 6, 1931, Greenlee Co., AZ. Entered Navy Sept. 6, 1950, NAS, Corpus Christi, TX. Assign-ments: NAS Moffett Field; USS *Philippine Sea* (CV-47).

Discharged June 28, 1954, Treasure Island, CA. Awards/Medals: UNSCV, U.S. Defense, GCM, PUC, Korean PUC, KSM w/7 Battle Stars, Chinese, Navy Occupation (Asia).

Married to Jeannie Beth Burrier, Aug. 12, 1955; no children. Retired USDA Soil Conservation Service, March 16, 1955-April 3, 1994; ranching/antique aircraft.

RONALD LLOYD STEPHENS, AT2, born Jan. 6, 1932. Entered USNR March 11, 1951 in Detroit, MI. Assignments: Hat Wing 1, NAS Norfolk, VA; VC-11; NAS, Miramar, San Diego, CA, HU2; USS *Philippine Sea*.

Memorable experiences include operations off the coast of Korea and how cold it was. Discharged March 11, 1960 from USNR, San Francisco, CA. Awards/Medals: GC, OCE, OCJ, CS, EPS, ND, KS, UN, KPUC.

Married with two sons and three granddaughters. Retired General Motors Sept. 1, 1986. He enjoys crafts and wood working.

ROBERT D. STEWART JR., AL3, born June 24, 1930, Meadville, PA. Parents moved shortly thereafter to Clarion County, PA. Raised on a farm near Reidsburg, PA and attended high school in Clarion, PA. Enlisted in USN June 22, 1948. Recruit training Great Lakes, IL; Aviation Elec tronics School Memphis, TN; Radar School, Norfolk, VA; brief assignment to Air Sqdn. at Quonset Point, RI NAS. Transferred V-2 Div. USS *Philippine Sea* spring of 1950. Main duty, Aviation Radio Shop & Primary Fly. Two tours to Korea.

Discharged June 3, 1952. Medals received include the UN Medal, KSM, Navy Occupation and China Service.

Attended Clarion State College, received ASC in police science from Salmon P. Chase College, Cincinnati, OH. Received MPA from University of Dayton, OH. During this period he worked 15 years in law enforcement in Clarion, PA, Silverton and Madeira, OH. Served 4-1/2 years as city manager of Madeira, OH and 15 years as city manager of Xenia, OH retiring in June of 1986. After retirement he served two years as economic development director for Xenia Area Chamber of Commerce and did part-time consulting.

In 1954 he married Yvonne Allison of Limestone, PA and they have six children, 11 grandchildren and two great-grandchildren. He enjoys spending time with his extended family, traveling, riding his 75 BMW, woodworking, computing, and dabbling in rental real estate and investments.

DALE STORMER, MM3, born Oct. 22, 1928, Empire, MI. Entered military Jan. 17, 1946; assignments at NTC, Great Lakes, IL; NTS Newport, RI, USS *Philippine Sea* (CV-47), RecSta, Brooklyn, NY.

Discharged Nov. 24, 1947, Receiving Station, Brooklyn, NY. Received the WWII Victory Medal.

Married Ruth and they have five sons, 15 grandchildren and eight great-grandchildren.

HENRY D. STRUVE, MM3/c, born Nov. 19, 1927, Utica, NY. Enlisted in the USN Jan. 4, 1946; Great Lakes boot camp followed by engineering training, Newport, RI. Member of the original crew of the USS Philippine Sea; plankowner, participated in her first sea voyage and her shakedown cruise to Guantanamo Bay, Cuba.

Departed Norfolk on Jan. 2, 1947 for Antarctica with ADM Byrd's Operation High Jump Task Force. Served in M Div., stood sea watches in the Forward Engine Room No. 1 throttle, main control. Discharged in November 1947.

Graduated SUNY College of Environmental Science and Forestry Class of 52, with a degree in engineering. Joined General Electric Co. and retired 36 years later as Rocky Mountain Regional Manager.

Married Mary Ellen Grady in 1955 and raised two great children. They currently reside in Englewood, CO. He enjoys travel, cruising, gardening, golf and his grandchildren. Volunteers at the Samaritan House for the homeless and is active in GE's Elfun Society, an organization of community service retirees.

KENNETH L. THOMAS, AN, born Nov. 6, 1932, Maysville, KY. Entered USN Sept. 13, 1950, Cincinnati, OH. Boot camp, Great Lakes Training Station, IL; USNAS Kwajalein; USNAS Alemeda; FASRON 8; CAG 9; USS *Philippine Sea* (CVA-47).

Memorable experiences include Task Force 77, VF-93 and Korean Hostilities. Discharged Sept. 3, 1953 USNS, Treasure Island, CA. Awards include the KSM w/3 stars and UN Medal.

He and wife, Marlene (Dozier) of Hamilton, OH, have five children: Kenneth II, Brian, Terry, Darryl and Marlak.

Attended Ohio University, Athens, OH, American Institute of Banking. Retired in 1991 from Star Banc with 35 years of service. He enjoys golfing, traveling, gardening, seeing his family, watching his grandchildren grow, watching TV and carpentry work.

BENJAMIN THOMPSON JR., SK1, born Sept. 21, 1928 in Medford, MA. He enlisted in the USN in June 1946 in Boston, MA. His recruit training took place at USNTC, Bainbridge, MD. He served on the USS *Philippine Sea* (CV-47) from 1946-1951 and was assigned to the USN ROTC staff at Dartmouth College where he served until he was honorably discharged in June 1954.

The highlight of his career was being a member of the ADM Richard Evelyn Byrd Antarctic Expedition in 1947.

Awards/Medals: GCM w/Bronze Star, WWIIVM, Navy Occupation Service Medal w/Europe Clasp, CSM (extended), NDSM, KSM w/star, Antarctica Service Medal, UNSM, NUCR Bar and ROKPUC.

Married Barbara Fraser in 1961. They have four children: Susan, Lauri, William and David.

Currently he serves as chairman of the board of trustees of Compensation Funds of New Hampshire and chairman of the Town of Hanover Republican Committee, as well as holding office as a trustee of New Hampshire Catholic Charities, Inc. He is presently employed as a hearing examiner for the State of New Hampshire Department of Safety.

In a public career that spanned more than 45 years, he served as a Hanover police officer, chief of police for the city of Lebanon, planner/coordinator for the Governor's Commission on Crime and Delinquency, and served three terms as a Hanover Selectman. In other public service positions, he served as special assistant to the late U.S. Senator Norris Cotton and as a member of the staff to the late U.S. Representative James C. Cleveland. He is co-founder of the USS *Philippine Sea* Association.

FRANK S. URBANOWICZ, TE2, born Aug. 14, 1925, Stamford, CN. He was drafted into the USNR-V6 in May 1944. Boot camp at Great Lakes was followed by a troop train ride to Treasure Island for assignment. A troop ship to Pearl was followed by a fleet oiler ride to the Mariannas area to catch the USS *Ralph Talbot* (DD-390). After a breeches ride while refueling, he settled into normal sea duty. That followed almost continuous duty with the 3rd, 4th, 5th, and 7th Fleets. He was discharged on May 2, 1946.

Recalled to active duty in December 1950 and reached the *Philippine Sea* while she was on duty off Korea. He was discharged May 17, 1952. Awards/Medals: American Area Ribbon, WWIIVM, Asiatic-Pacific Ribbon w/8 stars, PLR w/2 stars, Japanese Occupation, CSM w/2 stars, Korean Ribbon, and UN Ribbon w/star.

He will never forget the people jumping into the sea at Guam, the typhoon that sank three destroyers, the sea battles off the Philippines, and the feeling when they crossed the "T" at Linguan Gulf. The feeling as they raised the flag at Iwo Jima, the shudder as the ship was struck by a kamikaze and the narrow miss by the second plane. Escorting the cruiser *Portland* to Truk Island for its surrender, going back to Nagasaki and going ashore for the mail and viewing the destruction from the atom bombs and their plane raids. Taking a captain aboard and going to Sasebo to take the surrender aboard ship and seeing the plight of the people. Also, the many friends he made aboard the *Philippine Sea* and to view the recovery of Japan from his last visit; being in the post office enabled him to make many friends.

Married Pearl Guzniczak on Aug. 7, 1948 in Chicago, IL. They celebrated their 50th anniversary in 1998. They have four wonderful children: Rosanne in Arizona, Margaret in Wisconsin, Gloria in South Dakota and Michael in Colorado They also have five grandchildren.

Worked 31 years for the Chicago Milwaukee Railroad until retiring in 1977 due to a neck injury. He became a Wisconsin State Building Inspector with seven licenses, then became a professional home inspector, retiring in 1994. Served as building inspector for Sharon and Clinton, WI, and also the city of Lake Geneva, WI. During this time was also the fire inspector, zoning administrator and served on the planning commission. He has been on the board of directors and is the supervisory chairman with the Harvard, IL Community Credit Union.

He has enjoyed camping, hiking, and traveling about the country to visit their children; going to Polka Festivals and reunions. He is active in the USS *Ralph Talbot* (DD-390) Association and will host their reunion to be held in Milwaukee this year.

PHILLIP J. WALKER, SSGT, born July 21, 1929, Pontiac, MI. Enlisted USMC July 1948 Detroit, MI; boot camp Parris Island, SC. After completion of Sea School, Portsmouth, VA transferred to the MarDet USS *Philippine Sea* at Quonset Point, RI, December 1948.

Transferred to Marine Barracks, Yokasuka, Japan, April 1951 for further transfer to Treasure Island, CA Marine barracks; transferred June 1951 to the USN retraining comm-and, Norfolk, VA until discharge July 1952. Medals include the GC, CSM, KSM, Navy Occupation and United Nations.

Spent one year at Michigan State College and three years in the USMCR. Entered Birmingham, MI Police Department, 1952-1956. Entered the Michigan State Police until retiring in January 1980.

Married and has three children. Since retiring has traveled extensively with wife, Nancy; currently resides in Harbor Springs, MI. Active in the Marine Corps League, American Legion and Kiwanis Club.

G. LLOYD WILLIAMS JR., AD2, born Dec. 29, 1928 in Seattle, WA. Graduated Tacoma High School (1947) Maple Valley, WA; attended Central Washington College, Ellensberg, WA, pre-law major. Joined the USN June 29, 1948; 1948-1949, USNTC, San Diego, CA for 13 weeks, NATTC Airman School Class P, eight weeks and Aviation Machinist Mate School Class A, 14 weeks, Memphis, TN (1949-1952).

Assigned to USN Attack Sqdn. 115, Carrier Air Group 11, Fleet Training Ship/Shore flight line, plane captain, NCO in charge, NAS North Island, San Diego, CA and USS *Philippine Sea* (CV-47). First Korean tour-plane captain July 1950-April 1951. Second Korean tour-flight line NCO December 1951-May 1951. Served on the flight deck on both tours in combat operations.

Discharged June 4, 1952 with the rank AD2. His awards include the KSM w/silver star, GCM, UNSM, NUCR, NDSM and the ROKPUC.

Earned BCS ATTG degree from Seattle University in 1957. Earned CPA license, California 1965 and Oregon 1994.

Employed 1957-1960 with IRS; 1960-1970 with CPA firm; 1970-1998 as owner-operator of his own CPA practice. Memberships include: Naval Memorial Foundation, VFW, Korean War Veterans Association, Association Naval Aviation, Naval Aviation Museum USS *Philippine Sea* Association (CV-47) The Chosen Few (Korea), Naval Institute, Navy League, American Veterans, Tailhook Association, American Legion, VA-115 Assoc. and also has several professional memberships.

Married 47 years with two children, three grandchildren and two great-grandchildren.

LEWIS ADRIAN WILLIAMS (HANK),

born Aug. 29, 1932 in Greenville, NC. Enlisted in USN Aug. 21, 1951. Following recruit training in San Diego, CA was assigned to the USS *Philippine Sea* as signalman. Transferred the summer of 1952 to the S-2 D Div. Served as a cook approximately three years. Was promoted to 3rd class commissaryman.

During his tenure he traveled fo the Philippines, Subic Bay; Manila; Hong Kong, China; Okinowa, Hapan; and Coast of Korea.

Married Phyllis Riggs July 6, 1957. They have a daughter, Gina; a son-in-law, Dean Picot; and three grandchildren: Chandler, Kristen and Jared Picot. Much time is spent with grandchildren and family.

He continues a family trade as brick mason and has been self-employed since 1965.

He and his wife of 41 years enjoy worshipping in a local Pentacostal Church where he plays the guitar. He and his wife enjoy traveling in their travel trailer and flounder fish gigging, boating when time permits.

JAMES L. WRIGHT,

born Oct. 18, 1927, New Baltimore, NY. Entered military Sept. 15, 1945 at New York, NY; discharged Oct. 18, 1948, NAAS, Charleston, RI.

Assignments: Fasron 5, Oceawa NAS, UF10A, Bainbridge boot camp, NATTC Jacksonville, NATC Memphis.

Awards/Medals: ATM, WWIIVM, GC and European Occupation.

Married and has four sons and seven grandchildren. Graduated from Oswego State in 1950 and worked as contractor and Indiana arts teacher, 1950-1982.

RUSSELL YOUNG,

AG3, born Nov. 24, 1937, New Haven, CT. Entered military Sept. 13, 1955 in New Haven, CT;

Assignments at Bainbridge, MD; Hutchinson, KS; Norman, OK; Lakehurst, NJ; USS *Philippine Sea* (CV-47), 1957; USS *Floyd Bay* (AVP-40), 1958; Far East service *Philippine Sea*, 1958, station ship Hong Kong, Floyds Bay.

Discharged Aug. 24, 1958, Treasure Island, San Francisco, CA.

We'd better make this play a short one?

Skippers of the USS Philippine Sea

RADM D.S. Cornwell, USN

RADM J.L. Pratt, USN

RADM R.R. Waller, USN

RADM W.K. Godney, USN

Skippers of the USS Philippine Sea

RADM I.E. Hobbs, USN

RADM A. Smith, Jr. USN

RADM P.H. Ramsey, USN

RADM W.S. Harris, USN

Skippers of the USS Philippine Sea

RADM H.L. Ray, USN

CAPT G.S. James, USN

CAPT L.L. Farrington, USN

RADM M.H. Tuttle, USN

Skippers of the USS Philippine Sea

CAPT J.G. Hedrick, USN

INDEX

A

Ahroon 29, 30
Alexander 32
Allen 51
Allender 56
Amen 18, 19, 20
Anderson 15, 49
Aslund 20
Atwell 57
Aycock 48

B

Baker 31
Barr 63
Benedetto 52
Benton 31
Bermudez 6
Birdsong 6
Blown 25
Boone 18
Bricker 51
Buerger 11
Bulwark 30
Butts 20
Byland 6
Byrd 13, 15, 45, 47, 51, 55, 65

C

Callahan 52
Carlovsky 30
Chandler 11
Clark 16, 22, 24
Clarke 6
Colby 51
Cook 38
Cooper 6
Coral Sea (CVB-43) 16
Cornwell 11, 13, 14, 55
Cossett 52
Cowan 30
Cressman 10
Crooks 28
Crow 18, 19, 20
Cruzen 65

D

Damian 28, 32
David 54
Decker 6
Deyo 11
Dietz 49
Dixon 49, 51
Doucet 51
Downing 23
Drewniak 49
Duncan 27, 31, 32

E

Epperson (DDE-719) 29
Essex (CVA-9) 24
Evans 6
Ewen 18

F

Farnworth 18
Farrington 28
Faucet 51
Felt 27
Ferrell 48
Fink 32
Foss 38
Franklin (AVT-8) 31
Franklin D. Roosevelt 16
Fullerton 65

G

Gaffrey 29, 30
Gallatin 6
Gallery 39
Goery 52
Goodney 18
Gough 6
Greene 60
Guyer 26

H

Hagen 48, 51
Hale 51
Hanko 51
Harris 24, 28, 29
Hart 51
Hatcher 6
Hawkes 14, 15, 55
Hayden 51
Hedrick 30
Heflin 65
Hewitt 48
Hill 6, 52
Hitchcock 49
HMS Triumph 16
Hobbs 20, 22, 28
Howell 6
Hrabica 49
Huebner 51
Hunt (DD-674) 27

I

Irwin 51
Ishee 49

J

Jackson 18, 19, 20
James 28
Jennings 14
Jester 6
Johansen 51
John R. Craig (DD-885) 29
Johnson 6, 38, 49

K

Kail 18
Kearns 52
Kingsley 29
Knight 38
Korsgren 31

Kropp 6

L

Lake 23
Lake Champlain (CVA-39) 24
Lane 53
LeBaron 31
Lehman 31
Leyte (AVT-10) 31
Leyte (CV-32) 20
Linn 15
Lund 53

M

Martin 15, 20
Mayer 6
McCool 52
McGinnis 51
Meacher 29
Meisel 53
Melbourne 30
Merrick 55
Miller 6, 49
Milner 11
Minnetonka (WPG-67) 30
Modica 39
Montgomery 65
Mount Olympus 55
Mundt 6
Murphy 49

N

New Jersey (BB-62) 21
Nixon 53
Northwind 55
Norton 49
Nugent 38, 54

O

Offerman 28
Oriskany (CV-34) 16
Owens 6

P

Packard 49
Parish 27
Phillips 6, 27, 28
Pope Pius XII 63
Pratt 14, 16
Pridham-Whipple 16
Princeton's VA-195 23

R

Raines 48, 49
Ramsey 24
Ranney 40, 41, 53, 54, 57
Ray 28
Renshaw (DDE-449) 29
Ribble 28, 32
Rizzoto 6
Rochford 28, 31, 32
Rowe (DD-564) 27

Rowney 23
Ruble 28

S

Salsig 28
Sanger 49, 51
Schiller 6
Shaw 48, 49
Siewert 41, 44, 59
Smith 19, 22, 24, 49
Sonenshein 49
Soucek 22
Stanley 30
Straner 52
Stratocruiser 30

T

Tatham 28, 32
Taylor 65
Tefft 6
Thomas 53
Thorin 39
Tieranzzano 38
Truman 65
Tuttle 28, 29, 30, 57

U

USCGC Northwind 14
USS Independence 49
USS Kearsage 65
USS Midway 59
USS Missouri 54, 56
USS Widham Bay 51
USS Williamberg 65
USS Wright 10, 12
Uszenski 6

V

Valley Forge (CV-45) 18, 20
van Deurs 14
Vardakis 49
Vogel 18, 19, 38

W

Wahlstrom 28, 32
Walker 53
Waller 16, 18, 25, 53, 54
Williams 6
Wilson 6
Wood 49
Wormsley 49
Wright 10, 48, 49

Y

Yokosuka CVA-47 28

Z

Zardus 32
Zivich 6